T0246801

INTEGRAL SOCIETY

Social Institutions and
Individual Sovereignty

"This is an excellent book. Based on Integral Theory, it demonstrates how to create a society that is more functional, ethical, economical, and otherwise more integral. I definitely recommend it very highly."
—Ken Wilber, *A Theory of Everything*

"Gordon Anderson builds on the philosophy of Ken Wilber to outline the contours of a more ethical and functional civilization. Anderson makes a convincing argument for the necessity of individual economic autonomy and the widespread distribution of capital."—Steve McIntosh, author of *Developmental Politics*

"Critical and constructive, bold and daring, *Integral Society* challenges 21st-century persons to think deeply about fundamental institutional changes needed to defend the sovereignty of individuals. This wide-ranging and debatable book advances inquiry and action toward those vital goals."—John K. Roth, Edward J. Sexton Professor Emeritus of Philosophy, Claremont McKenna College

"Gordon Anderson has given us a remarkably readable history of the roots of integral society and its potential future. Along the way he discloses and illustrates the real faults, gnarls, and blockages of such a society for today's world."—Allan Combs, Professor of Consciousness Studies, California Institute of Integral Studies, author *The Radiance of being: Understanding the Grand Integral Vision; Living the Integral Life*

"In *Integral Society* Gordon Anderson argues that there is a purpose to human history which is the realization of free and resilient individuals in societies coordinated by institutions of which they are masters, not slaves. The author sees this as glimpsed at key moments in the past and within our grasp today to make a permanent state if we but have the courage to face down the systemic evils in our midst.—Don Trubshaw, co-founder of Societal Values website and coauthor of *Freedom and Belonging*

INTEGRAL SOCIETY

Social Institutions and Individual Sovereignty

by

Gordon L. Anderson

PARAGON HOUSE

First Edition 2023

Published in the United States by
Paragon House
www.paragonhouse.com

Copyright © 2023 by Gordon L. Anderson

All rights reserved. No part of this book may be reproduced, in any form, without written permission from the publisher, unless by a reviewer who wishes to quote brief passages.

Library of Congress Cataloging-in-Publication Data

Names: Anderson, Gordon L., (Gordon Louis), 1947- author.
Title: Integral society : social institutions and individual sovereignty /
   by Gordon L Anderson.
Description: First edition. | [Saint Paul] : Paragon House, 2023. |
   Includes bibliographical references and index. | Summary: "This book is
   a manifesto for an integral society, a society in which sovereign
   individuals are served by social institutions not exploited by them.
   Banking and investment firm cabals have engaged in unchecked forms of
   theft that distribute "new money" to wealthy elites and governments.
   Universities, the news media, corporations, and government agencies have
   been hijacked by financial interests, manias, and ideologies that
   exploit the sovereign individuals they were created to serve. Social
   institutions have a valuable place in an integral society, but they must
   be kept to their mission, sphere, and level of society. This book is
   about creating governance systems that do this so that sovereign
   individuals are able to pursue life, liberty, and happiness in a
   sustainable world"-- Provided by publisher.
Identifiers: LCCN 2022051239 (print) | LCCN 2022051240 (ebook) | ISBN
   9781557789495 (paperback) | ISBN 9781610831314 (epub)
Subjects: LCSH: Social integration. | Social institutions. | Individualism.
Classification: LCC HM683 .A534 2023 (print) | LCC HM683 (ebook) | DDC
   306--dc23/eng/20221222
LC record available at https://lccn.loc.gov/2022051239
LC ebook record available at https://lccn.loc.gov/2022051240

The paper used in this publication meets the minimum requirements of American National Standard for Information Sciences—Permanence of Paper for Printed Library Materials, ANSIZ39.48-1984.

Manufactured in the United States of America
10 9 8 7 6 5 4 3 2 1

For those who would build societies where life, liberty, and happiness is pursued by all.

CONTENTS

Introduction: Integral Society

Societies have become very complex since early nation-states formed in the 17th century. Corporations, central banks, political parties, government bureaucracies and many other social institutions have arisen to assert great control over individual citizens. These institutions can be of great service or harm to individuals, depending on their purpose and how well they are managed. Will a way be found to keep them in the service of the people, or will they create a dystopian future in which people have little value except as serfs to those who control these institutions?

Much of the strife in our societies results from the loss of freedom and personal sovereignty as social institutions expand, taking control of governments, land, food, money, health, and energy. Self-sufficient individuals, small businesses, and small towns are threatened by wealthy elites, global financial conglomerates, and the financial, ideological, and political hijacking of institutions. Inflation, the fear of rigged elections, and energy shortages are causing populist uprisings as those who control the governments, banks, and resources threaten them with indignity.

We have reached a critical point in the evolution of human society. The array of highly developed social institutions in our complex post-modern world can either be put to the service of individual sovereignty and happiness or, left unchecked, put to the service of elites who use these institutions for their own power and wealth as sovereign citizens become a new type of feudal serf.

This book is intended to show the way forward and stimulate discussion on how to to achieve an integral society. In an integral society, social institutions exist for specific purposes that serve human beings. Integral society is created by an integral consciousness. That consciousness is rooted in a view of the whole that respects the value of each individual.

Integral consciousness is developing in our world as reflection on the nature and purpose of our post-modern life accelerates. The most popular pioneer in the field of integral studies is Ken Wilber, whose *A Theory of Everything: An Integral Vision for Business, Politics, Science and Spirituality*[1] was a best seller. The California Institute for Integral Studies (CIIS) was named in 1980 to "strives to embody spirit, intellect, and wisdom in service to individuals, communities, and the earth."[2] CIIS describes integral studies as "a response to the growing need to synthesize the fragmentary aspects of contemporary thought and culture into a meaningful whole."[3]

Allan Combs, who teaches at CIIS, describes the developing integral vision in *The Radiance of Being: Understanding the Grand Integral Vision; Living the Integral Life.*[4] The foreword is by Ken Wilber. Steve McIntosh applied this vision to widen our understanding of modern philosophy in his book *Integral Consciousness and the Future of Evolution.*[5] Paul Smith applied integral theory to the evolution of Christianity in *Integral Christianity: The Spirit's call to Evolve.*[6]

The articulation of the integral vision is not the purpose of this book, but a brief diagrammatic overview is provided in the Appendix. In this book, integral theory is applied to the study of society and social institutions to address critical social problems of our time, the relationship between sovereign individuals and social institutions.

Social institutions exist at different levels, spheres, and stages of consciousness. They are not "conscious" the way human beings are, but they have purposes and values that form the institutional culture. The family is the most basic human institution, a combination of biological necessity and organized human cooperation. Societal levels advance from family

---

1. Ken Wilber, *A Theory of Everything: An Integral Vision for Business, Politics, Science and Spirituality,* (Boston: Shambhala, 2000).

2. About CIIS, https://www.ciis.edu/about-ciis

3. Ibid.

4. Allan Combs, *The Radiance of Being: Understanding the Grand Integral Vision; Living the Integral Life* (St. Paul, MN: Paragon House, 2002).

5. Steve McIntosh, *Integral Consciousness and the Future of Evolution* (St. Paul, MN: Paragon House, 2007).

6. Paul Smith, *Integral Christianity: The Spirit's Call to Evolve* (St. Paul, MN: Paragon House, 2011).

to community, town, city, county, state, regional federations of states, and the world. The three basic spheres of society are culture, economy, and governance.

An integral society is based on a principled relationship between culture, economy, and governance. Each social sphere and its institutions are rooted in different principles that must be differentiated, understood, and integrated into complex postmodern societies.

The three primary spheres of society are based on three spontaneous orders that evolve in any human community—language, money, and law.[7] Language, money, and law refer to culture, economy, and governance, respectively. Frederick A. Hayek, developing the thought of Bernard Mandeville, David Hume, Adam Smith, and Carl Menger, discussed how three social orders develop naturally and spontaneously in all types of human society and all stages of human social evolution.

The cultural sphere is primary. It shapes human consciousness by transmitting values, goals, and knowledge that enable individuals to pursue relationships, economic necessities, and a good life. The sphere of culture is based on the pursuit of love, truth, beauty, and goodness. The family, schools, arts, sports, and other social institutions enable the individual's pursuit of happiness.

The economic sphere is necessary to support our biological life and is often where we serve others. Money and markets arise spontaneously due to the desire to produce, exchange, and share things that enable us to live and pursue other goals. Economic institutions like factories, stores, banks, and services arise to serve these needs.

The sphere of governance is necessary to referee disputes in relationships and competition for the use of resources. The sphere of governance involves rules like "thou shall not steal" and "thou shall not kill" that enable people to pursue happiness in a secure and harmonious society. Police, governors, judges, courts, legislatures, and other institutions of

---

7. James U. Blanchard III and F. A. Hayek, "Exclusive Interview with F.A. Hayek," Cato Institute Policy Report, May-June 1984. https://www.cato.org/policy-report/may/june-1984/exclusive-interview-fa-hayek#

governance arise to maintain social order so that individuals can pursue happiness in the cultural and economic spheres.

In an integral society, the social institutions in all three spheres perform different and complementary roles to serve all human beings in pursuing a good life that does not infringe on others' rights to pursue happiness. An individual human being has many organs of the body that serve necessary and complementary functions. A healthy individual is an integral biological system. Social institutions are the organs of society. They much each perform there function in a way that serves both the individual and society. In an integral society, each social organ performs its function.

THE EVOLUTION OF HUMAN SOCIETY

Human society has evolved from hunter-gatherer societies to large complex civilizations with many social institutions in each sphere. Human consciousness has developed with this evolution of society. The evolution of this consciousness is the centerpiece of Ken Wilber's *Theory of Everything*. While this evolution has an overall development we can trace over the last 12,000 years, it is not determinate or guaranteed. Civilizations have risen and fallen based on social consciousness, motivations of leaders, and the nature of social institutions.

Hunter-gatherer consciousness is closer to animals that graze and hunt for food. Warfare and tribalism are byproducts of human societies subsisting on natural resources in competition with others.

Civilization is rooted in the production of goods and services adequate for everyone. There is no need to fight over goods, but cooperation in their production and distribution is necessary. Civilization requires governing a social order where killing and stealing are forbidden. The role of government shifts from organizing military conquests to securing borders and protecting private property. Cultural institutions transmit the rules and skills necessary to live peacefully and prosperously. The socialization process involves the suppression and control of animal instinct. Problems of shortages are not solved by theft and violence but with inventiveness and skills aimed at the production and delivery of more goods and services.

The origins of civilization are generally traced to agriculture and the domestication of animals in ancient Mesopotamia and Turkey. Yet, the animal instincts to plunder and kill remain submerged, appearing in random personal acts of violence, conquest, theft, and slavery. Cultural institutions remain challenged to adapt as new technologies, financial, and governance institutions are created in increasingly complex societies. People can use new developments for good or evil purposes if they are not understood and restrained by society. Institutional actors increasingly influence social behavior.

Knowledge has advanced from superstitious beliefs to sophisticated science and philosophy embedded in corporations and universities. Economic institutions have evolved from personal businesses to the mergers and acquisitions controlled by investment firms. Governance institutions have expanded from tribes to states, federations, and global institutions with agencies created to regulate all kinds of human activity.

This book discusses the evolution from simple nation-states to federations of states and what Ken Wilber has labeled "integral commons."[8] The founding of the United States represents the first modern effort of social evolution from a system of simple states run by kings or governors to Constitutional Republics in which sovereign individuals are free to pursue happiness through a more sophisticated interplay of social institutions. The security of states and their relations is governed by a federal system of checks and balances on power designed to allow individuals to pursue happiness freely.

THE NATURE OF INDIVIDUALS AND INSTITUTIONS

The history of modern political theory begins with the realism of Nicolo Machiavelli. Machiavelli's *Prince* was a discourse on how princes could maximize their power. In modern societies with complex institutions

---

8. See Figure 6 in the Appendix. Ken Wilber, *A Theory of Everything: An Integral Vision for Business, Politics, Science, and Spirituality* (Boston: Shambhala, 2001).

of governance, versions of this type of governance, strategic realism, are found in the planning by government agencies like the U.S–CIA, Russia's SVR, and China's MMS. They seek to maximize state interests and consider individuals exploitable and expendable. They act in secret and without accountability to individual citizens.

Thomas Hobbes, the founder of modern political science, was a realist who argued for a social contract. His realism consisted in viewing human beings as driven by survival instincts where "the state of nature is a state of war."[9] Society is naturally brutish and requires strong governments to keep people in line. In *Leviathan,* he argued that individuals should cede control to an institutional sovereign who would work for them according to a social contract approved by the citizens. He had a realistic view of human nature but an undeveloped view of the nature of social institutions.

August Comte, the founder of modern social science, was an idealist who believed human beings naturally loved one another and that evil existed in society. He blamed traditional religions and cultures for promoting superstitions and lies that turned people against each other and argued that tradition could be replaced by social science. Karl Marx accepted Comte's premises and, in *Capital,* argued that modern economic institutions and processes were the sources of evil, exploitation, and class consciousness. Unlike Hobbes, Marx's idealism viewed ancient communal societies with the kind of nostalgia Christians view the world of Adam and Eve before the fall.

Post-modernism promotes the view that truth is relative. It cannot be found in either the traditional world of Hobbes or the scientific world of Comte. Neither religious nor scientific knowledge are free from teachers and researchers' biases and cultural prejudices. Everything is rooted in the narratives that dominate social consciousness. This has led to a view called constructivism in which the world is viewed as socially constructed. Constructivism sees culture as primary in society, contrary to

---

9. "State of Nature," *Encyclopedia Britannica.* https://www.britannica.com/topic/state-of-nature-political-theory.

the realist and liberal theories that focus on material factors like power and money.

An integral approach sees truth and blind spots in all these theoretical perspectives. For example, Marxists see evil in social institutions but ignore individual human nature. They throw out the baby with the bathwater. Debates that pit Christians against Marxists, Realists against Liberals, Conservatives against Progressives, or Rights against Responsibilities are spurred by levels of social consciousness that fail to see a broader integral perspective.

Human beings are born with natural instincts and a consciousness that is socialized. We are capable of transcending inherited consciousness and the socially constructed realities in which we live. We also form social institutions. Some are spontaneous and rooted in the social instincts to communicate, exchange, and create rules. Others are organized and socially constructed. These institutions can either serve or exploit individuals. Both individuals and social institutions have good or evil potential that depends on the level of personal consciousness and social consciousness they attain.

INDIVIDUAL SOVEREIGNTY IN A WORLD OF INSTITUTIONS

Individual sovereignty lies at the foundation of an integral society. Social institutions have more power, wealth, or knowledge than individuals. But they are composed of individuals who have individual consciousness. This consciousness is limited to sense experience and instinct at birth and shaped by socialization and the desire to pursue well-being, family life, truth, beauty, and goodness. Individuals create social institutions to facilitate this pursuit.

Individual sovereignty is at the basis of spontaneous social orders. We create language to communicate, exchange goods and services for mutual benefit, and create rules to live with each other. People at all times and places do these things. Good rules and social institutions will serve the natural pursuits of sovereign individuals. "Do not kill" is a social rule that enables everyone to live their life. "Do not steal" enables personal economic sovereignty by allowing people to control the property they will need to live or exchange with others. "Do not lie" promotes the natural role of language communication. These basic rules support personal sovereignty and the spontaneous orders at the base of the three spheres of society. They are necessary for an integral society.

Social organizations are mostly planned institutions rather than spontaneous natural orders.[10] These two types of social phenomena, planned and unplanned, contribute to social evolution and an integral society. However, planned institutions that create rules impeding personal sovereignty cause human suffering and eventually fail. Such institutions would be considered evil.

The story of the tower of Babel illustrates social organization is not possible if the people cannot communicate. Centrally planned economies fail because individuals are not free to produce and exchange desired products. States fail when elites use power to serve their own ends rather than enabling people's pursuit of happiness. These social institutions fail when the try to suppress the spontaneous social orders that spring from human nature.

In an integral society, planned social institutions have natural limits imposed by the requirements of society's spontaneous evolutionary nature. Integral social consciousness understands this. When a lower level of consciousness attempts to manage social institutions, they get hijacked for personal ends, misdirected for ideological purposes, or acquired by other institutions. Hijacked institutions fail to serve individuals and the whole of society.

The great religions and modern psychology have laid down guidelines for personal self-control and rules for interaction with other individuals. Similar advice and regulations have not been adequately developed for social institutions. This is the nature of the manifesto embedded in this book. A declaration of integral society and a proposed constitution for an integral society are presented to develop the integral consciousness

---

10. Friedrich A. Hayek, *The Road to Serfdom*, University of Chicago Press, 2007 (originally 1944).

required to govern modern social institutions. Existing social institutions in all three spheres can be made more effective when focused on their mission, kept in their place, and appropriately limited by law.

OUTLINE OF THIS BOOK

Part 1 presents a Declaration and Constitution of an integral society. The Declaration begins with a statement on individual sovereignty and human rights and responsibilities. It then lists ways social institutions have deprived individuals of these rights and caused human suffering. Particularly banks and political parties must be better governed.

This is followed by a proposed Constitution designed to check the abuses and corruption of both individuals and social institutions, enabling people to pursue happiness. This Constitution updates the United States Constitution, but is designed to stimulate discussion on the updating of any constitution for a regional level federation of states. Many of the proposed articles apply to states also. A Constitution is the legal operating system of a society and requires the type of vigilance found in computer software updates when hackers and viruses exploit weaknesses.

Parts 2 and 3 serve the same purpose for the Constitution of an Integral Society as the Federalist Papers in explaining the articles of the U.S. Constitution. It draws on successes and failure of the past, showing glimpses of an integral society in previous societies and the nature of abuses of power and money.

Part 2 discusses the evolution of civilization from the world of survival instincts described by Thomas Hobbes as "the state of nature" through the rise of civilization and evolution of individuals with the possibility of autonomy in all three social spheres. Individual sovereignty in Ancient Babylon and Rome is explained and show how that sovereignty was lost in the collapse of the Roman Empire into feudalism and the dark ages.

Part 3 examines the rebirth of individual sovereignty in city-states, widespread education, and the Protestant Reformation, lay the foundations of self-responsibility. Widespread individual sovereignty existed in the 18th century when the U.S. Founders created a governance system for free people. This was followed by the rise of science, technologies, and new social institutions. However, an anarchic "state of nature" developed among social institutions that often hunt, prey on, and devour the sovereign individuals they initially rose to serve. New types of institutional tribalism and warfare in culture, economy, and government are a result.

The rise of modern banking and government/bank cabals has deprived individuals of their economic autonomy, concentrating capital in the hands of a few. Laws that give everyone an equal opportunity to own and profit from new capital are the most-needed development in the 21st century. The concentrations of power and wealth in social institutions must be limited and under the control of the people those social institutions should serve.

In the legislative arena, it is important to remove the role of political parties as vehicles for social institutions and wealth in lawmaking, and return political power to the citizens. There are other more debatable suggestions made for getting qualified and politically neutral government administrators. Civil service exams, lotteries, and other methods of avoiding the appointment of unqualified political cronies are suggested.

Finally, the Appendix contains diagrams by Wilber and Anderson that help illustrate the nature, evolution, and complexity of an integral society. is attached.

Part 1

A Constitution for an Integral Society

Chapter
1

Declaration of an Integral Society

PREAMBLE TO A CONSTITUTION

The Preamble to the Constitution is a statement of purpose and vision. It describes the common goals, assumptions, and principles that inform the Constitution's making. In the United States, the Declaration of Independence serves this purpose in greater detail than the first paragraph of the Constitution.

Every social organization benefits from a vision statement and by-laws. In a modern, complex, integral society, these purposes should be focused and limited so as not to wander outside their social sphere or harm or dominate other institutions or sovereign individuals. Further, the government has a role in serving as a referee of social institutions and individuals.

The United States Constitution was drafted at a stage of social evolution before the rise of the complex social institutions we have today. Modern banks and corporations were in their infancy. Religion and the press were guaranteed freedoms, but their power constrained. The U.S. Founders did an excellent job creating "a more perfect" government than previous governments, but they compromised on slavery and did not enfranchise women. Those were two problems rectified later, after social protest and war.

Other problems exist today. The period 1776 to 2022 saw social evolution go from early nations (stage 4) to the entry of integral commons (stage 7) on Ken Wilber's diagram (Figure 6) in the Appendix. A

Preamble to a post-modern Constitution has to address new concentrations of power and wealth and conflicts of interest. As the founders thought integrally in their day, most of their work should stand with corrections and additions to account for social changes.

The proposed declaration of an integral society can serve as a preamble for a Constitution of an Integral Society.

DECLARATION OF AN INTEGRAL SOCIETY

From time to time, the evolution of society requires a social compact appropriate to its people and social institutions. Human society has evolved from clans to tribes, to feudal empires, nation-states, corporate states, and value communities. It now stands at the forefront of an integral commons.

States, corporations, and value communities have created social institutions that serve sovereign human beings. These institutions have been insufficiently governed and have often been turned into vehicles for wealth, power, and control, destroying individual sovereignty. The abuse and misuse of social institutions must be restrained.

We hold that each human being is a sovereign individual with a consciousness capable of transcendence in search of Truth, Beauty, Goodness, and the Pursuit of Happiness.

We hold that to facilitate this pursuit, each human being has a right to love, to family, to association with others, to own property, to acquire knowledge, to make and sell products and services. These rights are not ultimate ends in themselves, but they are intermediate ends and a fundamental means to enable individuals to pursue happiness.

We hold each right bears a corresponding responsibility. In interacting with society and nature to promote one's perfection, every person must respect other human beings and the rest of creation. Each person is responsible for pursuing truth and values, and to promote economic and social justice.

We hold that each human being, a steward of nature, remains responsible for living in harmony with nature, which is interdependent and the foundation of the existence of human beings.

We hold that, to secure these rights and responsibilities, governments are instituted among people, deriving their just powers from the consent of the governed. Whenever any government or other social institution becomes destructive of these ends, it is the right of the people to alter or to abolish it, laying its foundation on the principles and form of organization most likely to effect their safety and happiness.

Prudence dictates that governments long established should not be changed for light and transient causes. Experience has shown that people are more disposed to suffer, while evils are sufferable, than to right themselves by abolishing the forms to which they are accustomed. But when a long train of abuses and usurpations, pursuing the same object evinces a design to force them under absolute despotism, it is their right and duty, to throw off such government and to provide new guards for their future security. Such has been the patient sufferance of the people under institutional abuse. Now necessity constrains them to alter their former systems of government.

We hold that an integral society consists of a complex interaction of social institutions in the spheres of culture, economy, and governance. These institutions have purposes and limits in their service to sovereign individuals. People create and maintain social institutions as highly specialized tools designed to serve social functions within a just social order. Institutions, as organized expressions of society's values and goals, affect the quality of each person's individual and social life. As historical creations of humanity carry within themselves the wounds of history, institutions are continually in need of healing and perfecting.

People create tools shaped from the resources and energies of nature to support the economic and social sovereignty of the person. Through private property ownership, everyone can become a master of the technology needed to realize their fullest human potential and dignity.

* * *

Today people have been deprived of the right to pass laws in the interest of sovereign citizens through corrupted processes of legislation controlled by political parties, moneyed interests, and the bureaucratic state.

They have failed to protect rights and secure borders.

They have violated the principle of subsidiarity and states rights.

They have entered into banking cabals that steal from depositors and provide independent financing for the government causing inflation as a hidden tax on the people.

They have appropriated resources from the integral commons rather than refereeing their use by the people.

They have created quasi-standing armies through agencies that do not represent the consent of the governed.

They have allowed mergers, acquisitions, and interlocking boards of corporations and institutions that overreach the limits and change the purposes of institutions, so they fail to help the citizens they were created to serve.

They have created intelligence agencies that lack accountability and engage in spying, entrapment, misuse of funds, black operations that violate the rights of people, and cover-up misdeeds through the classification of documents the citizens have a right to see.

They have created independent sources of funding to escape accountability to legislatures.

They have passed laws encouraging the concentration of capital rather than wide distribution among sovereign citizens.

They have censored the speech of those pursuing truth.

They have erected a multitude of new offices and sent hither swarms of officers to harass our people and eat out their substance.

They have combined with others to subject us to a jurisdiction foreign to our constitution and unacknowledged by our laws.

They have improperly confined citizens and failed to provide them with speedy and fair trials.

They have cut off the trade of citizens with many parts of the world.

They have imposed taxes that violate the principle of subsidiarity.

They have deprived us, in many cases, of the benefits of Trial by Jury.

They have taken away charters, abolished the most valuable laws, and fundamentally altered the forms of our governments.

They have suspended citizens from conducting business or legal processes in the name of emergencies.

They have excited domestic violence and theft and advocated policies that harm life and liberty.

We have petitioned for redress in the most humble terms: Our repeated petitions have been answered only by repeated injury. Officials whose character is marked by every act that may define a tyrant are unfit to rule a free people or their social institutions.

We have appealed to the native justice and magnanimity of ruling elites, and we have conjured them by the ties of our common kindred to disavow these usurpations, which would inevitably interrupt our connections and correspondence. They, too have been deaf to the voice of justice and consanguinity.

* * *

We, therefore, declare our intent to end the unjust practices of governments, agencies, banks, and other social institutions that deny or impede the fundamental rights and responsibilities of sovereign individuals in their pursuit of life, liberty, and happiness.

With the goal of social evolution, not revolution, we put forward a proposed Constitution of an Integral Society. With the recognition that human society has evolved from early nations states to societies of complex social institutions, we believe that adjustments to the Constitution of the United States can serve as the foundation, as that Constitution evolved from governance systems that preceded it.

With the goal of social evolution, not revolution, we put forward the proposed Constitution for a Federation of States. It is not a system of law to be imposed by force or military imposition, but by the voluntary consensus of peoples and leaders who will to serve the sovereignty of others. We desire to create a more perfect government standing on the successes of the past and guarding against future harm to individuals.

Chapter 2

A Constitution for an Integral Society

We, the People of an Integral Federation of States,[1] to form a more perfect union, establish justice, insure domestic tranquility, provide for the common defense, promote the general welfare, and secure the blessings of liberty to ourselves and our posterity, do ordain and establish this Constitution.[2]

ARTICLE. I. LEGISLATIVE BRANCH

Section. 1.

All legislative Powers herein granted shall be vested in a Congress of the Federation, which shall consist of a Senate and a House of Representatives.

Section. 2.

The House of Representatives shall be composed of Members chosen through election by the people of the several States, as determined by their State Legislature. The term shall be four years.

---

1. These governance principles refer to any federation of states in which the sovereign rights and responsibilities of individuals are upheld.

2. Note that these articles include suggestions by the author to address problems discussed in this book. They are intended for discussion in the evolution of constitutional thought as other factors not discussed or known or better solutions could lead to changes. The author believes approval of a constitution by more than three-fourths of the population represents the consent of the governed. The *Federalist Papers* contributed to such debate at the U.S. Founding.

No person shall be a Representative who shall not have attained to the Age of thirty years and been seven years a citizen of the Federation, and when elected, be an inhabitant of that State in which he shall be chosen.

Representatives and direct taxes shall be apportioned among the states that may be included within this Federation, according to their respective numbers. The actual enumeration shall be made within three years after the first meeting of the Congress within every subsequent term of ten years. No enumeration will include religion, race, party, or other group affiliation. There shall not be less than two hundred Representatives, nor more than one Representative for every fifty thousand persons.

Immediately after they shall be assembled in consequence of the first election, they shall be divided into two classes as equally as may be possible. The representative seats' of the first class shall be vacated at the expiration of the second year, and of the second class at the expiration of the fourth year so that one-half may be chosen every second year.

If vacancies happen by resignation or otherwise, the executive authority shall issue a special election to fill such vacancies.

The House of Representatives shall choose its Speaker and other Officers; and shall have the sole Power of Impeachment.

Section. 3.

The Senate of the Federation shall be composed of two Senators from each State, chosen by the Legislature thereof, for six years, and each Senator shall have one vote.

Immediately after they shall be assembled in consequence of the first Election, they shall be divided into three classes as equally as possible. The seats of the senators of the first class shall be vacated at the expiration of the second year, of the second class at the expiration of the fourth year, and the third class at the expiration of the sixth year, so that one-third may be chosen every second year. If vacancies happen by resignation, or otherwise, during the recess of the Legislature of any State, the executive thereof may make temporary appointments until the next meeting of the Legislature, which shall then fill such vacancies.

No person shall be a Senator who shall not have attained to the Age of thirty-five years and been nine years a citizen of the Federation, and shall be an inhabitant of that State for which he shall be chosen.

The Federation's Vice President shall be President of the Senate, but shall have no vote, unless they are equally divided.

The Senate shall choose their other officers and also a president *pro tempore* in the absence of the Vice President or when he shall exercise the Office of President.

The Senate shall have the sole power to try all Impeachments. When sitting for that purpose, they shall be on Oath or Affirmation. When the President of the Federation is tried, the Chief Justice shall preside: And no Person shall be convicted without the Concurrence of two-thirds of the Members present.

Judgment in cases of Impeachment shall not extend further than to removal from office and disqualification to hold and enjoy any office of honor, trust, or profit under the Federation: but the party convicted shall nevertheless be liable and subject to indictment, trial, judgment, and punishment, according to law.

Section. 4.

The times, places, and manner of holding elections for senators and representatives shall be prescribed in each state by the Legislature thereof.

The Congress shall assemble at least once every year.

Section. 5.

Each House shall be the judge of the elections, returns, and qualifications of its members, and a majority of each shall constitute a quorum to do business. A smaller number may adjourn from day to day and may be authorized to compel the attendance of absent members, in such manner, and under such penalties, as each House may provide.

Each House shall pass no bill with more than one subject and no less than a two-thirds majority of votes.

Each House may determine the other rules of its proceedings, punish its members for disorderly behavior, and expel a member with the concurrence of two-thirds.

Each House shall keep a journal of its proceedings and from time to time publish the same, excepting such parts as may in their judgment require secrecy. The yeas and nays of the members of either House on any question shall, at the desire of one-fifth of those present, be entered on the journal.

Neither House, during the session of Congress, shall, without the consent of the other, adjourn for more than three days, nor to any other place than which the two Houses are sitting.

Section. 6.

The Federation will provide offices for Senators and Representatives but shall not provide compensation for their services from the Treasury of the Federation. Congress shall pass no bill regarding the salaries of the members or their staff or appropriate money, therefore. All such expenses must be borne by the states they represent.

They shall in all cases, except treason, felony, and breach of the peace, be privileged from arrest during their attendance at the session of their respective Houses, and in going to and returning from the same. For any speech or debate in either House, they shall not be questioned in any other place.

Members of Congress may not accept any money or payment from any lobbying organization or institution while in office. They must recuse themselves from voting on any item that engenders a personal conflict of financial interest under penalty of a fine as determined by law. Nor shall Members or their immediate family purchase stock in any corporation while Congress is in session.

No Senator or Representative shall, during the time for which he was elected, be appointed to any civil office under the authority of the Federation, which shall have been created, or the emoluments whereof shall have been increased during such time. No person holding any office under the Federation shall be a Member of either House during Continuance in Office.

Section. 7.

All Bills for raising Revenue shall originate in the House of Representatives, but the Senate may propose or concur with Amendments as on other Bills.

Every Bill which shall have passed the House of Representatives and the Senate, shall, before it becomes a Law, be presented to the President of the Federation. If the President approves shall sign it, but if not shall return it, with written objections to that House in which it shall have originated, who shall enter the objections at large on their journal, and proceed to reconsider it. If after such Reconsideration, three-fourths of that House shall agree to pass the Bill, it shall be sent, together with the objections, to the other House, by which it shall likewise be reconsidered, and if approved by three-fourths of that House, it shall become a Law. But in all such cases the votes of both Houses shall be determined by yeas and nays, and the names of the persons voting for and against the Bill shall be entered on the Journal of each House respectively. If any Bill is not be returned by the President within ten Days (Sundays excepted) after it has been presented, it shall be a law as if the President had signed it, unless the Congress by their Adjournment prevent its return, in which case it shall not be a law.

Every order, resolution, or vote to which the concurrence of the Senate and House of Representatives may be necessary (except on a question of adjournment) shall be presented to the President of the Federation. Before the same shall take effect, shall be approved by him, or being disapproved by him, shall be repassed by three-fourths of the Senate and House of Representatives, according to the rules and limitations prescribed in the case of a Bill.

Section. 8.

The Congress shall have the power to lay and collect taxes, duties, imposts and, excises, to pay the debts and provide for the common defense and general welfare of the Federation; but all duties, imposts, and excises shall be uniform throughout the Federation;

To borrow money on the credit of the Federation; except from a Central Bank that controls the creation of new money.

To regulate commerce with foreign nations and among the several states;

To promote the progress of science and useful arts by securing for limited times to authors and inventors the exclusive copyrights and patents to their respective writings and discoveries. Such rights shall only be held by individual citizens not corporations or other social institutions. Their duration shall not last beyond seventeen years;

To constitute tribunals inferior to the supreme court;

To define and punish piracies and felonies committed on the high seas and offenses against the law of nations;

To declare war, grant letters of marque and reprisal, and make rules concerning captures on land and water;

To raise and support armies, except for standing armies or arming domestic agencies, but no appropriation of money to that use shall be for a longer term than two years;

To provide and maintain a navy;

To make rules for the government and regulation of the land and naval forces;

To provide for calling forth the militia to execute the laws of the union, suppress insurrections, and repel invasions;

To provide for organizing, arming, and disciplining, the militia, and for governing such part of them as may be employed in the service of the federation. The appointment of the officers and the authority of training shall be reserved to the states respectively according to the discipline prescribed by congress;

To exercise exclusive legislation in all cases whatsoever, over such district (not exceeding ten miles square) as may, by the cession of particular states and the acceptance of Congress, become the seat of the Government of the Federation, and to exercise like authority over all places purchased by the consent of the Legislature of the state in which the same shall be, for the erection of forts, magazines, arsenals, dock-yards, and other needful buildings;—and

To make all laws which shall be necessary and proper for carrying into execution the foregoing powers, and all other powers vested by this constitution in the government of the federation, or in any department or officer thereof, except laws that violate other sections of this Constitution.

Section. 9.

The migration or importation of such persons as any of the states now existing shall think proper to admit shall not be prohibited by the congress. However, a tax or duty may be imposed on such importation, not exceeding one hundred dollars for each person.

The privilege of the writ of habeas corpus shall not be suspended unless, when in cases of rebellion or invasion, the public safety may require it.

No bill of attainder or ex post facto law shall be passed.

No arms shall be issued to federal employees for domestic use. Local or state police or militias shall provide protection if they deem it necessary. The Federation shall only issue arms to the military, including protection for the President, who is its Commander in Chief.

To establish a uniform rule of naturalization,

The Federation shall grant no title of nobility. No person holding any office of profit or trust under them, shall, without the consent of the Congress, accept of any present, emolument, office, or title, of any kind whatever, from any king, prince, or foreign state.

Section. 10.

No state shall enter into any treaty, alliance, or confederation; grant letters of marque and reprisal; coin money; emit bills of credit; make any thing but gold and silver coin a tender in payment of debts; pass any bill of attainder, ex post facto law, or law impairing the obligation of contracts, or grant any title of nobility.

No state shall, without the consent of Congress, lay any imposts or duties on imports or exports, except what may be absolutely necessary for executing its inspection laws. The net produce of all duties and imposts, laid by any state on imports or exports, shall be for the use of the treasury of the Federation, and all such laws shall be subject to the revision and control of the Congress.

No state shall, without the consent of Congress, lay any duty of tonnage, keep troops, or ships of war in time of peace, enter into any agreement or compact with another state or with a foreign power, or engage in war, unless invaded, or in imminent danger as will not admit of delay.

ARTICLE. II. EXECUTIVE BRANCH

Section. 1.

The executive power shall be vested in a President of the Federation. The President's term of office shall be four years, and, together with the Vice President, chosen for the same term, be elected as follows:

Each state shall appoint, in such manner as the Legislature thereof may direct, a number of electors equal to the whole number of senators and representatives to which the state may be entitled in the congress: but no senator or representative, or person holding an office of trust or profit under the federation, shall be appointed an elector.

The electors shall meet in their respective states and vote by ballot for two persons, of whom one at least shall not be an inhabitant of the same state with themselves. And they shall make a list of all the persons voted for, and of the number of votes for each; which list they shall sign and certify, and transmit sealed to the seat of the government of the Federation, directed to the President of the Senate. The President of the Senate shall, in the Presence of the Senate and House of Representatives, open all the certificates, and the votes shall then be counted. The person having the greatest number of votes shall be the President, if such number be a majority of the whole number of electors appointed; and if there be more than one who have such majority, and have an equal number of votes, then the House of Representatives shall immediately choose by ballot one of them for President; and if no person have a majority, then from the five highest on the list the said House shall in like manner choose the President. But in choosing the President, the votes shall be taken by States, the representation from each State having one vote; A quorum for this Purpose shall consist of a member or members from two-thirds of the States, and a majority of all the States shall be necessary to a choice. In every case, after the choice of the President, the person having the greatest number of votes of the electors shall be the Vice President. But if there should remain two or more who have equal votes, the Senate shall choose from them by ballot the Vice President.

The Congress may determine the time of choosing the electors and the day on which they shall give their votes; which day shall be the same throughout the Federation.

No Person except a natural born Citizen, or a Citizen of the Federation, at the time of the adoption of this Constitution shall be eligible to the office of President; neither shall any person be eligible to that office who shall not have attained to the age of thirty-five years, and been fourteen years a resident within the Federation.

In case of the removal of the President from office, or of his death, resignation, or inability to discharge the powers and duties of the said office, the same shall devolve on the Vice President, and the Congress may by law provide for the case of removal, death, resignation or inability, both of the President and Vice President, declaring what officer shall then act as President, and such officer shall act accordingly until the disability be removed, or a President shall be elected.

The President shall receive for services, compensation, which shall neither be increased nor diminished during the term of office. No other emolument from the Federation or the States shall be given during the term of office.

Before entering on the Execution of his Office, the President shall take the following oath or affirmation:—"I do solemnly swear (or affirm) that I will faithfully execute the Office of President of the Federation, and will to the best of my ability, preserve, protect and defend the Constitution of the Federation."

Section. 2.

The President shall be Commander in Chief of the Army and Navy of the Federation and of the militia of the several states when called into the actual service of the Federation. The President may require the opinion, in writing, of the principal officer in each of the executive departments, upon any subject relating to the duties of their respective offices, and shall have Power to grant reprieves and pardons for offenses against the Federation, except in cases of Impeachment.

The President shall have Power, by and with the advice and consent of the Senate, to make treaties, provided two-thirds of the Senators present concur; and he shall nominate, and by and with the advice and consent of the Senate, shall appoint Ambassadors, consuls, and all other officers of the Federation, whose appointments are not herein otherwise provided for, and which shall be established by law: but the Congress may by law vest the appointment of such inferior officers, as they think proper, in the President alone, in the courts of law, or in the heads of departments.

The President shall have the power to fill up all vacancies that may happen during the recess of the Senate by granting commissions that shall expire at the end of their next session.

Section. 3.

The President shall, from time to time, give to the Congress information of the State of the Union and recommend to their consideration such Measures as he shall judge necessary and expedient; he may, on extraordinary occasions, convene both Houses or either of them, and in case of disagreement between them, concerning the time of adjournment, he may adjourn them to such time as he shall think proper; he shall receive Ambassadors and other public ministers; he shall take care that the Laws be faithfully executed, and shall Commission all the officers of the Federation. The President may issue executive orders to departments in his role of executing the laws, but they do not have the force of law. Congress may overturn any executive order.

Section. 4.

The President, Vice President, and all civil officers of the Federation, shall be removed from office on Impeachment for, and conviction of, treason, bribery, or other high crimes and misdemeanors.

Section 5.

Public Ministers who are heads of Federation Departments and agencies must be qualified for their position as determined by law. They are accountable to the President, who is the chief administrator, but have a primary duty to administer the department as directed by laws established by Congress.

Public Ministers shall be chosen by lottery from among candidates submitted by the States. Each state may submit one candidate.

Section. 6.

The transparency of all government institutions is necessary for citizen oversight. No government department may classify information to hide spending or other activities except for military security. Classified documents will be declassified after a time of seven years. The punishment for false classification of documents shall be removed from office.

ARTICLE III. THE JUDICIARY

Section. 1.

The judicial power of the Federation shall be vested in one Supreme Court consisting of nine justices and in such inferior courts as the Congress may from time to time ordain and establish. The judges, both of the supreme and inferior courts, shall hold their offices during good behavior, and shall, at stated times, receive compensation for their services, which shall not be diminished during their continuance in office.

Supreme Court justices shall be chosen by lottery from candidates submitted by the states, with only one submission per state. Candidates should be qualified in constitutional law and be a minimum of thirty-five years of age. The Vice President will conduct the lottery within ninety days of a vacancy. The term of a Supreme Court justice shall expire when the justice reaches an age of eighty years or upon resignation or removal by impeachment.

Section. 2.

The judicial power shall extend to all cases, in law and equity, arising under this Constitution, the laws of the Federation, and treaties made, or which shall be made, under their authority;—to all cases affecting Ambassadors, other public Ministers and Consuls;—to all Cases of admiralty and maritime Jurisdiction;—to controversies to which the Federation shall be a Party;—to controversies between two or more States;— between a State and Citizens of another State,—between Citizens of different States,— between Citizens of the same State claiming Lands under Grants of different States, and between a State, or the Citizens thereof, and foreign States, Citizens or Subjects.

In all Cases affecting Ambassadors, other public Ministers and Consuls, and those in which a State shall be Party, the Supreme Court shall have original jurisdiction. In all the other cases mentioned before, the Supreme Court shall have appellate jurisdiction, both as to law and fact, with such exceptions and under such regulations as Congress shall make.

The trial of all crimes, except in cases of impeachment, shall be by jury; and such trial shall be held in the state where the said crimes shall have been committed; but when not committed within any state, the trial shall be at such place or places as the Congress may by law have directed.

Section. 3.

Treason against the Federation shall consist only in levying war against them or in adhering to their enemies, giving them aid and comfort. No person shall be convicted of treason unless on the testimony of two witnesses to the same overt act or on confession in open court.

The Congress shall have the power to declare the punishment of Treason, but no Attainder of Treason shall work Corruption of Blood or Forfeiture except during the Life of the Person attainted.

ARTICLE. IV. THE STATES

Section. 1.

Full faith and credit shall be given in each state to the public acts, records, and judicial proceedings of every other state. And the Congress may by general laws prescribe how such acts, records, and proceedings shall be proved, and the effect thereof.

Section. 2.

The citizens of each State shall be entitled to all privileges and immunities of citizens in the several States.

A person charged in any state with treason, felony, or other crime, who shall flee from justice, and be found in another state, shall on demand of the executive authority of the state from which he fled, be delivered up, to be removed to the state having jurisdiction of the crime.

No person held to service or labor in one state, under the laws thereof, escaping into another, shall, in consequence of any law or regulation therein, be discharged from such service or labor, but shall be delivered up on claim of the party to whom such service or labor may be due.

Section. 3.

Congress may admit new States into this Federation; but no new State shall be formed or erected within the Jurisdiction of any other State; nor any State be formed by the junction of two or more states, or parts of states, without the consent of the Legislatures of the States concerned.

The Congress shall have the power to dispose of and make all needful rules and regulations respecting the territory or other property belonging to the Federation; nothing in this Constitution shall be so construed as to prejudice any claims of the Federation, or of any particular state.

Section. 4.

The Federation shall guarantee to every State in this union a republican form of government and shall protect each of them against invasion; and on the application of the Legislature or of the executive (when the Legislature cannot be convened) against domestic violence.

Section. 5.

States are guaranteed a right to secede with the consent of three-fourths of their citizens and with no less than ninety days notice to the Federation. If requested, Federal property in a departing State must be returned or paid for by a duly assessed fair market value.

Section. 6.

The powers not delegated to the United States by the Constitution, nor prohibited by it to the States, are reserved to the States respectively or to the people.

ARTICLE V. THE CITIZENS

Section. 1.

A well-regulated Militia, being necessary to the security of a free State, the right of the people to keep and bear Arms, shall not be infringed.

Section. 2.

No Soldier or federal agent shall, in time of peace, be quartered in any house, without the consent of the owner, nor in time of war, but in a manner to be prescribed by law.

Section. 3.

The right of the people to be secure in their persons, Houses, papers, and effects, against unreasonable searches and seizures, shall not be violated. No Warrants shall issue, but upon probable cause, supported by Oath or affirmation, and particularly describing the place to be searched, and the persons or things to be seized.

Section. 4.

No person shall be held to answer for a capital, or otherwise infamous crime, unless on a presentment or indictment of a Grand Jury, except in cases arising in the land or naval forces or in the Militia, when in actual service in time of War or public danger. No person subject for the same offence shall be twice put in jeopardy of life or limb. No person shall be compelled in any criminal case to be a witness against himself, nor be deprived of life, liberty, or property, without due process of law; nor shall private property be taken for public use, without just compensation.

Section. 5.

In all criminal prosecutions, the accused shall enjoy the right to a speedy and public trial by an impartial jury of the State and district wherein the crime shall have been committed, which district shall have been previously ascertained by law, and to be informed of the nature and cause of the accusation; to be confronted with the witnesses against him; to have compulsory process for obtaining witnesses in his favor, and to have the Assistance of Counsel for his defense.

Section. 6.

In suits at common law, where the value in controversy shall exceed twenty dollars, the right of trial by jury shall be preserved, and no fact tried by a jury shall be otherwise re-examined in any Court of the United States than according to the rules of the common law.

Section. 7.

Excessive bail shall not be required, nor excessive fines imposed, nor cruel and unusual punishments inflicted.

Section. 8.

The enumeration in the Constitution, of certain rights, shall not be construed to deny or disparage others retained by the people.

ARTICLE VI. MONEY, TAXES, AND BANKING

Section. 1.

A central bank shall have the power to coin money, regulate the value thereof and of foreign coin, and fix the standard of weights and measures;

To provide for the punishment of counterfeiting the securities and current coin of the federation;

The central bank may act as an exchange bank or clearing house but may not issue loans.

Congress shall not borrow money from the central bank;

Congress may authorize the Treasury to issue bonds for sale to individual citizens, but no government bonds shall be owned by banks, corporations, or other social institutions.

Section. 2.

No capitation or other direct tax shall be laid unless in proportion to the census or enumeration herein before directed to be taken. Such taxes will be paid by the States, not directly by the Citizens. All direct taxes and income taxes on Citizens will be collected and managed by the States.

No tax or duty shall be laid on articles exported from any state to another in the Federation.

Any regulation of commerce or revenue shall give no preference to the ports of one state over those of another: nor shall vessels bound to, or from, one state, be obliged to enter, clear, or pay duties in another.

Section. 3.

Neither Congress nor the States shall tax the profits of any corporation, religion, or other social institution. Such profits must be paid to the owners and shareholders or reinvested in production. All taxes shall be levied on the individual income derived from profits or through payments of wages or dividends. Congress or the States may mandate a minimum distribution of profit of up to 50 percent to owners and shareholders. Social institutions shall be incorporated in the states and not under the jurisdiction of the Federation, except for the regulation of interstate commerce. Social institutions may be limited in scope and purpose by the State charter.

No money shall be drawn from the treasury, but in consequence of appropriations made by law. A regular statement and account of the receipts and expenditures of all public money shall be published annually.

There shall be uniform laws on the subject of bankruptcies throughout the Federation.

ARTICLE. VII. SOCIAL INSTITUTIONS

Section. 1.

Congress shall make no law respecting an establishment of religion, political party, cultural association, or other organization or prohibiting the free exercise thereof. Congress shall not abridge the freedom of assembly.

No census shall be allowed to question or categorize people by s cultural, racial, or political identity, nor shall public databases classify individuals by any group affiliation. No ballot shall list the religion, political party, or another cultural identity group next to the names of candidates. The government will not appropriate any funds for political party primaries, or other political activities of private organizations or candidates.

Section. 2.

Congress shall not abridge the freedom of speech, or of the press; and to petition the Federation for a redress of grievances. The Federation shall issue official reports as established by law, but shall not establish or support any news media, entertainment programming, or other social media. Nor shall any government department dictate the censorship of any topic in the press.

ARTICLE. VIII. AMENDMENTS

Section. 1.

The Congress, whenever two-thirds of both Houses shall deem it necessary, shall propose Amendments to this Constitution, or, on the application of the Legislatures of two-thirds of the several states, shall call a convention for proposing amendments, which, in either case, shall be valid to all intents and purposes, as part of this constitution, when ratified by the Legislatures of three-fourths of the several states, or by conventions in three fourths thereof, as the one or the other mode of ratification may be proposed by the Congress; and that no State, without its Consent, shall be deprived of its equal Suffrage in the Senate.

ARTICLE. IX. CONTINUANCE OF OBLIGATIONS

Section. 1.

All Debts contracted and Engagements entered into, before the Adoption of this Constitution shall be as valid against the Federation under this Constitution as under the previous Constitution.

This Constitution, and the laws of the Federation which shall be made in pursuance thereof; and all treaties made, or which shall be made, under the authority of the Federation, shall be the supreme law of the land; and the judges in every state shall be bound thereby, anything in the constitution or laws of any state to the contrary notwithstanding.

The senators and representatives before mentioned, and the members of the several state Legislatures, and all executive and judicial officers, both of the Federation and of the several States, shall be bound by oath or affirmation, to support this Constitution. No religious, racial, sexual, or other identity group test shall ever be required as a qualification to any office or public trust under the Federation.

ARTICLE. X. RATIFICATION

Section. 1.

The Ratification of the Conventions of three-fourths of the States shall be sufficient for the Establishment of this Constitution between the States so ratifying the Same.

Part 2

The Evolution of Society

Chapter
3

The State of Nature: Predator or Prey

> The "natural condition of mankind" is what would exist if there were no government, no civilization, no laws, and no common power to restrain human nature. The state of nature is a "war of all against all," in which human beings constantly seek to destroy each other in an incessant pursuit for power. Life in the state of nature is "nasty, brutish and short."[1]
> —Thomas Hobbes

The state of nature described by Thomas Hobbes (1588-1679) is the starting point for studying politics and society. Hobbes is considered the "father of modern political philosophy"[2] and a pioneer in modern social science and morals. In the "state of nature," there is theft and murder, no security, no production and exchange, no peace, no culture, no social institutions, and no society. An integral society has the opposite: security, a prosperous economy, culture, social institutions, a sustainable environment, and happiness for all.

Both Hobbes' state of nature and an integral society are ideal types. The state of nature is a description of no social organization. Integral

---

1. Sparknotes summary of "The state of nature" in Thomas Hobbes' *Leviathan.* https://www.sparknotes.com/philosophy/leviathan/terms/

2. Garrath Williams, "Thomas Hobbes: Moral and Political Philosophy" *Internet Encyclopedia of Philosophy.* https://iep.utm.edu/hobmoral/#H1. Many refer to Nicolo Machiavelli, who lived a century earlier as the founder of modern political thought, but his work was more practical political advice to rulers than a work of philosophy.

society is a description of perfect social organization. Neither type of society exists in reality. Even in the brutish state of nature, cavemen with clubs had families they provided for and protected. People within groups cooperated. From there, history provides an understanding of the evolution of society, with advances and setbacks, from a brutish, uncivilized world to a modern, technically advanced, complex society. An ideal society is elusive; as technology and new social institutions evolve, people find new ways to use them to exploit and oppress others before rules of equal opportunity are developed. As Reinhold Niebuhr stated, the ideal is a goal "beyond history."[3] We can aim at a perfect society, but human life's finite and limited nature prevents us from achieving a perfect society in history.

THE BIOLOGICAL BASIS OF HUMAN LIFE

Human beings are first and fundamentally *biological beings*. Individual survival requires food, sleep, shelter, and security. Survival instincts are at the root of our unsocialized behavior. Any social science that ignores this will fail. A fundamental weakness in all social theories is the assumption that an ideal society will emerge if some oppressive social institutions are destroyed. Those oppressive social institutions are the product of human beings with biological instincts that must be socialized.

Secondly, humans are *social beings* by nature. Nature provides the instinctual drive for reproduction and companionship. The biological development of the body and brain outside the womb requires individuals to be nurtured by others for several years. Hobbes' view of a state of war of all against all has to be qualified by recognizing some human relationships and socialization processes will always exist, or the human race will not survive. These are what Hayek called spontaneous orders.

Thirdly, human beings are *rational* beings. The biological brain develops the ability to remember, compare, and reason. Rational reflection on the world produces knowledge, strategies to achieve goals, and the creativity to produce goods and services.

---

3. Reinhold Niebuhr, *The Nature and Destiny of Man, Volume II, Human Destiny* (New York: Scribner's, 1964), pp. 3ff.

The above three aspects of human nature exist to some extent in all societies. Hunter-gatherer societies rely on taking from what already exists, while civilization suppresses the urge to take and instead stimulates the production of goods and services. Warring barbaric tribes of hunter-gatherers are the closest type of society to Hobbes' description of "the state of nature."

HUNTER-GATHERER SOCIETY

Hunter-gatherer societies organize around a life of survival in the natural world. They forage for food, gather fruits, vegetables, and nuts, or hunt for meat. They find shelter in caves or make huts from sticks, grass, mud, or animal hides. The supply of food available by nature limits the population of hunter-gatherer societies.

Hunter-gatherers are predators or prey, like the animals they hunt. They are vulnerable to wolves, lions, or other hunting animals. And they are vulnerable to other people and tribes competing for natural food and resources. This is the state of nature.

Hunter-gatherer societies, small and large, exist in all three social spheres: cultural, economic, and governance. They display the spontaneous emergence of language, trading, and rules. Their practices make sense from the perspective of complete dependence on nature, but they seem cruel to those in civilized societies.

Hunter-Gatherer Economy

Foraging and hunting are activities of taking. While this is not "stealing" from other people, it is still taking from nature and not production. Such societies have rules about how the food is divided. However, the society as a whole depends on nature to provide food.

A hunter-gather economy can be considered a win-lose economy. Since there are limited resources, the person who finds a thing wins, and the others lose because it is unavailable. Food limitations inevitably cause fighting and death than can be avoided with abundance.

Hunter-Gatherer Culture

Hunter-gatherer culture defines social roles and rules centered on biological traits, skills, and the group's survival. Reason and technology improve hunting and gathering techniques, preparing food, and producing shelter. Rites of passage from childhood to adulthood signify learning and mastering adult tasks.

The culture of hunter-gatherer societies responds to the economic constraints of dependence on nature. The size of the population is limited by what nature can provide. It is suicide for a society to over-forage. Praying to nature for rain and thanking the animals for their life would not be considered superstition by a hunter-gatherer society. It is a sign of respect for the wildlife they depend upon.

The love that develops from relationships in the family and tribe creates a consciousness that transcends individual survival instincts. Behavior towards others in the group is cooperative, while behavior towards other groups will be competitive. Hunter-gatherer life is the source of in-group/out-group thinking that manifests when groups compete over resources. This in-group/out-group thinking exists today in political parties that hunt, gather, and compete for money in government treasuries. Lobbying is a modern form of hunter-gather activity, as are wars for conquest and plunder.

Hunter-Gather Governance

The leader in a hunter-gatherer society will often be the strongest person, and his primary role is protecting everyone. As leaders age, they become elders who retain wisdom for governance based on their experience.

A hunter-gatherer society will most value those who can hunt, gather food, and provide protection. Because only a limited amount of people can be supported by nature in a given territory, laws are created to determine who lives and dies to avoid mass starvation. Hunter-gatherer societies frequently sacrifice infants, virgin females, elders,[4] and the

---

4. This is commonly discussed in reference to the Inuit, who maintained this practice up until 1939. In ancient Japan was a practice known as *ubasute*, "granny dumping.

handicapped. An alternative practice is to force expulsion or abandon-
ment of children, the handicapped, or the aged. While these practices
may seem cruel and heartless, they are necessary for survival in societies
that hunt and forage rather than produce their food.

CRIMINAL GANGS

Criminal gangs in modern societies share many of the characteristics of
hunter-gather societies. Instead of hunting for wild food, they hunt for
money or other things to steal from wider society, using violence if necessary. Gang members provide for their families, as do tribal members.

Protection rackets for homes and businesses are common forms of
social parasitism when gangs are stronger than the local police. Modern
gangs exist in societies that are partly productive and partly predators.

INSTITUTIONAL HIJACKING

Another form of theft or parasitism involves the takeover of a social
institution and using its power and resources to serve oneself or a group.
Whether the institution is a hospital, a government, a corporation, or a
school in the cultural, economic, or political sphere, it has money and
resources. This money, and even the institution's employees, can be redirected by the hijackers.

Hijacking social institutions can be a takeover by force, but most
often, it is a takeover of the leadership from within by people with economic or ideological motives. There are many examples of children inher-
iting family businesses, squandering the capital, and causing bankruptcy,
either out of selfishness or ignorance. More typical today are corporate
raiders who legally acquire a company to take profits for itself or even
purposely put it out of business to eliminate competition and create a
monopoly that can exploit consumers.

A government agency or not-for-profit corporation is more likely to
suffer an ideological takeover than a financial acquisition because they do
not produce products for sale. However, they still have financial resources
and power that can be redirected. For example, the resources of a church

created for spiritual nourishment and care of the sick might be used for social activism.

Institutional hijacking is a form of predation that sees institutions as the prey. A good example is a Marxist call to "seize the means of production," in other words, to takeover corporations by force. Criminal gangs and hijackers of social institutions are not literally hunter-gathers dependent on nature. Instead, they are social dependents who prey on sovereign people or institutional resources and assets rather than natural resources. These are still selfish and uncivilized actions from biological survival impulses to take rather than social impulses to produce.

Chapter 4

Civilization: Production for All

Civilization: "a relatively high level of cultural and technological development specifically: the stage of cultural development at which writing and the keeping of written records is attained."

—Merriam-Webster Dictionary

CIVILIZATION REQUIRES PRODUCTION OF FOOD

This standard definition of civilization does not mention production but that writing and record-keeping are the fruits of production. Civilization could arise because food production replaced dependence on hunting and gathering and the limited population it could support. Food security allowed for the social division of labor, permanent homes, markets, and transportation and enabled many to pursue knowledge, inventions, and more comfortable life.

Historians trace the origins of Western Civilization to ancient Mesopotamia, Turkey, and Egypt.[1] Agrarian societies needed to protect farmers and land from warring invaders. The land had to be allocated or sold to owners. Houses and ownership of other property were publicly recognized and respected. Writing and record-keeping became necessary

---

1. "Agriculture in the Fertile Crescent & Mesopotamia," World History Encyclopedia. https://www.worldhistory.org/article/9/agriculture-in-the-fertile-crescent--mesopotamia/

to document ownership of property and contracts for goods and services to be produced or traded.

Agricultural societies supported large numbers of people and cities. Their size transcended the face-to-face interpersonal relations of tribal society, where everyone knew each other. Rules for wider impersonal life, bureaucracy, police, and courts emerged to enable commerce, safe travel, and settle disputes. Common language, impartial justice, and anonymous money for trade emerged, enabling the rise of vast empires. All this was made possible by moving from hunter-gatherer society to the organized production of goods and services.

Civilization transcended the "state of nature" in all social spheres:

1. In the *cultural sphere*, a common language, writing, and record-keeping expanded communication and knowledge. Many animal instincts are replaced or suppressed. Behavioral norms and rules for marriage, property, and trade developed, Tribal loyalties declined, and people of different tribal backgrounds would trade and intermarry. Temples arose with large tracts of land that produced food for cities. They also served as religious and cultural centers, organizing festivities and serving as communities of transition and welfare for widows, orphans, refugees, and the disabled.

2. In the *economic sphere*, the money, weights and measures, and markets and trade routes emerged for exchange and distribution of goods and services. Professional skills developed as farmers, artisans, business people, scribes, soldiers, and others engaged in specialized occupations. Agriculture used manual labor and oxen pulling plows. Slaves, refugees, and indentured labor formed part of the workforce, but some slaves earned freedom and became quire wealthy

3. The *governance sphere* needed to provide secure the borders and enforce laws against murder and theft at the minimum. There were also laws related to marriage, slavery, and taxes.

Hammurabi's Code and the Bible contain legal and cultural rules related to transitioning from hunter-gatherer society to agricultural civilization. The Bible begins with Adam and Eve being cast out of the garden to till the soil. The commandments against killing and stealing are essential to a civilized society.

BABYLONIAN EMPIRE: FEDERATION 1.0

Early empires in Mesopotamia arose with the stable production of food and other goods and services. The term "feudal empires" in Wilber's description of social evolution (listed as stage 4 in Figure 6, Appendix 1) misrepresents many of the early empires but describes the empires that emerged after the collapse of the Roman Empire. Many early empires had large numbers of citizens with great freedom and independence. This varied significantly depending on the ruler and the time.

The earth could only support about 10 million human beings if all were hunter-gatherers.[2] One scientific report puts the earth's population at 8,000 B.C., before the rise of civilizations, at about 5 million people,[3] and that at 100 C.E. at the height of the Roman Empire, there were about 300 million people on earth.[4] This 60-fold increase was made possible by an economy based on production and distribution.

From 4,000 B.C. to 2,000 B.C. the farming communities and towns in ancient Mesopotamia evolved from local rule, with military leaders fighting over control, to more centralized control. This civilization flowered under King Hammurabi (c. 1810–1750 B.C.) as he brought together a standard set of laws and a more uniform administration. In this sense, it was a federation of states with a complex social organization that is useful to study for integral society.

2. Joseph R. Burgera and Trevor S. Fristo,"Hunter-gatherer populations inform-modern ecology,' PNAS, February 6, 2018 (vol. 115|no.), p. 1138. https://www.pnas.org/content/pnas/115/6/1137.full.pdf.

3. Toshiko Kaneda and Carl Haub, "How Many People Have Ever Lived on Earth?" PRB, Jan. 23, 2020. https://www.prb.org/howmanypeoplehaveeverlivedonearth/.

4. Ibid.

Hammurabi was considered a good king who lived for the sake of his people. The Hammurabi Code[5] was a comprehensive set of rules covering murder, theft, false accusations, marriage and family, business, taxes, and slavery. This code is distilled in the Ten Commandments.[6] Punishments were harsh—an eye for an eye—and people obeyed. A stone stele with Hammurabi's code engraved is on display in the Louvre in Paris.

Hammurabi's code protected life, family, and property. This is essential for the long-term survival of any society. Hayek discussed this in his writings:

> It is interesting that, among the founders of religions over the last two thousand years, many have opposed property and the family. But the only religions that have survived are those which support property and the family.[7]

We now know a lot about Babylonian society because of the rules, activities, and transactions recorded on thousands of cuneiform tablets discovered in the 19th and 20th centuries.[8]

Governance

Hammurabi's Code makes the role of government primarily that of protector and referee, even though it is a governance system based on the laws promulgated by a king and attributed to the god of Babylon, Marduk.[9] This attribution to a transcendent authority meant that government officials were also subject to the same laws, and justice was not

---

5. https://avalon.law.yale.edu/ancient/hamframe.asp.

6. W.W. Davies, *The Codes of Hammurabi and Moses* (Cincinnati: Jennings and Graham, 1905).

7. F. A. Hayek, "The Presumption of Reason," prepared for the Plenary Address, 14th International Conference on the Unity of the Sciences, Houston, Texas, 1985. https://blog.ganderson.us/articles/the-presumption-of-reason/.

8. Gwendoyln Leick, *The Babylonians* (London and New York: Routledge, 2003), pp. 92-95.

9. In *Life, Liberty, and the Pursuit of Happiness, Version 4.0* (Paragon House, 2009), I referred to the form of governance of the Babylonian Empire as Version 1.0.

two-tiered. However, some punishments were harsher when violations were against state property.[10]

All three social spheres—government, economy, and culture—were under one ruler. However, Hammurabi allowed significant self-rule of city-states and citizens. His rules did not suppress the spontaneous orders of language and the market, and his laws served the individual pursuit of happiness within their bounds.

Hammurabi did not arbitrarily make up his code. It was a uniform standard created by integrating the laws that had evolved from the time of Sargon of Akkad (r. 2334-2279 B.C.) until that of his father Sin-Muballit (r. 1748-1729 B.C.). The code integrated Sumerian and Semitic traditions. "The code was advanced far beyond tribal custom and recognized no blood feud, private retribution, or marriage by capture."[11] The king, businesses, and temples had scribes who recorded laws and records. Hammurabi had copies of his laws carved on stones and put in major cities.

The absolute power held by a king meant he could impose arbitrary, capricious, or evil laws. However, his legitimacy was necessary for a peaceful rule. Looking back on previous government systems, Aristotle thought the best form of government was the rule of a good king that served the common good,[12] but if a king lost the consent of the governed, the regime would become a tyranny—the worst form of government. Hammurabi's rule was considered exemplary

ECONOMY

Babylon had irrigation systems that could provide a continuous flow of water to crops in dry seasons and agriculture on temple and palace lands that produced enough food for everyone in the cities to buy in markets.

---

10. For example: "If any one steal cattle or sheep, or an ass, or a pig or a goat, if it belong to a god or to the court, the thief shall pay thirtyfold therefor; if they belonged to a freed man of the king he shall pay tenfold; if the thief has nothing with which to pay he shall be put to death."

11. Johannes M. Renger, "Code of Hammurabi," *Encyclopedia Brittanica,* https://www.britannica.com/topic/Code-of-Hammurabi

12. Aristotle, *The Politics,* https://iep.utm.edu/aristotle-politics/#SH9c.

Farming was labor-intensive without modern machines like tractors, although oxen, plows, and other tools aided production. Some lands were centrally administered, employed local families, and used slaves. Some private farmers owned their land and paid for access to water.

Slaves and indentured servants could be used in the fields because there was also enough food for them. Hunter-gathers routinely killed rival tribes and some of their members because of food scarcity. However, civilized empires did not have to kill an enemy if they could be captured and put in useful work.

Slavery was part of Babylonian society but very different from modern stereotypes of slavery. Slavery was more like working off debt than capture and imprisonment. People could sell themselves into slavery and earn their freedom. As human beings, slaves had rights, could own property and businesses, and kept their families intact. If a master bought a married man, he also had to buy his wife and children. Slaves were usually the same race as their masters and worshiped the same gods. Slaves were treated as members of the family and educated to the same level.[13] Slaves were the property of masters and forced to work, but their jobs could be any form of labor—a laborer in the fields, a servant, a tradesman, or a literate scribe. Rules regarding slaves were complex because they could intermarry and share children and households with free people. However, their portion of household possessions went to their masters on their death, while the free spouse kept their possessions, and the children were free.

A productive economy with markets and trade enables a win-win situation for producers and buyers. Such win-win relationships are essential for social peace. Babylon protected the flourishing of free and fair markets. Hammurabi's Code outlined proper business relations and compensation and punishments for violations. The Code emphasized one's responsibility. A builder of a house that collapsed had to cover all damages. The manager of an irrigation dam that broke had to compensate all

---

13. *Slavery in Babylonia,* https://ililarbel.weebly.com/the-golden-rule-the-life-of-hillel-the-elder/slavery-in-babylonia

the farmers whose crops were damaged. Weights and measures were used for sales, and cheating was punished by law.

Hammurabi inherited a money system of barley and silver exchanged in units called shekels. The first coins did not appear until about 600 B.C. in Lydia. The Code of Hammurabi did specify monetary practices in which grain should be the currency used to pay for hired farmers or beasts of burden. In contrast, silver was used to hire doctors, artisans, or builders.

Private property was important and divided into movable (furniture, jewelry, animal, gold, and textiles) and unmovable (land and houses). "Fields" were land with access to water where food could be grown. Citizens had houses, plots of land for farming, or shops for business. Many necessities of modern life existed in Babylonian civilization.

CULTURE

The Babylonian language was the *lingua franca* of the entire Near East from the 15th to 13th centuries B.C.[14] Individual responsibility was the most important aspect of Babylonian culture. Laws assumed adults were responsible and harsh when people harmed others. Babylonian temples were more than religious institutions; they produced much of the food for the cities and performed services of social welfare. Temples were associated with deities, rituals, and festivals. They were responsible for the care of widows, orphans, the homeless, refugees, the sick, and the poor.

Temples were surrounded by large tracts of land used for productive farming and self-sufficiency. Extra food was sold to provide income for the temple and its residents. Residents of the temples lived communally. While temples sold most of the food they produced, portions were set aside "for the gods" and eventually, after a ceremony, were divided among the residents.

Residents of temples engaged in basket-weaving, silver-smithing, and other trades they learned as apprentices in the temples. They sold these products in front of the temples or at markets. Residents kept a portion

---

14. Gwendoyln Leick, *The Babylonians*, p. 50

of the proceeds and eventually, with skills and savings, moved out of the temple. They would get their own home or work for a wealthier family as a slave. This welfare-to-work program incentivized temple residents to become productive. It was an opportunity to move up the social ladder to become a free citizen.

Temples were not always self-supporting, and donations from the King, local officials, and other citizens were encouraged. This was a significant purpose for feast days when donations were collected.

THE ARBITRARY POWER OF A KING

Many Ancient Empires provided better lives for citizens than hunter-gather societies. But, their success was highly dependent on the character and skill of the ruler. A wise and good king, with just laws and secure borders, enabled citizens to pursue happiness and live full lives. But the people's fate was tied to the king's temperament and skills. Kings could be inept and unjust and could as likely be a tyrant as a benevolent overseers.

In *The Politics,* Aristotle, writing in the 4th-century B.C., provided some of the best analyses of ancient governments. Ancient people in city-states and empires experienced many kinds of rule: kings, tyrants, oligarchies, democracies, and mobs. Some systems lasted hundreds of years, while others failed quickly. Success or failure depended foremost on leadership skills and the virtue of leaders, but it also depended on the stability and resilience of the economy and culture.

In the Babylonian Empire, city-states' governance was semi-autonomous, and the economic and cultural spheres quite free. If the king changed, or even if a foreign king occupied the palace, much of the average citizen's life went on as normal. Individual sovereignty was significantly protected, and citizens were, for the most part, responsible for their own lives.

Aristotle described the difference between a king and tyrant. A king served at the pleasure of the people, whereas the people served the pleasure of a tyrant. The same is true of any government leader. When leaders use a government for themselves rather than the citizens, they sow the seeds of revolution:

> The beginnings of change are the same in monarchies as in forms of constitutional government; subjects attack their sovereigns out of fear or contempt, or because they have been unjustly treated by them. And of injustice, the most common form is insult, another is confiscation of property.[15]

Regardless of the form of government, the growth of populations is determined mainly by the economy. The most important factors in the transforming from a hunter-gatherer society to a civilized society are economic production, ownership of property, and markets. By "hunter-gatherer society," we can include groups that live by taking rather than producing. This includes criminal gangs, political parties, and other non-productive organizations plunder rather than produce.

Regardless of the form of government, the happiness of populations is determined mainly by the citizens' moral consciousness: their sense of freedom, responsibility, self-sufficiency

The force of government power, the strength of the economic market, and the force of cultural responsibility are all interrelated factors in the evolution of civilization. Ancient economy and culture were suited for the pursuit of happiness, and the lives of people were most likely disrupted by kings and leaders corrupted by power. Checks against the misuse of power were necessary for the next evolution in human society, which developed in the Roman Republic.

---

15. Aristotle, *The Politics*, Book V, Part X. http://classics.mit.edu/Aristotle/politics.5.five.html.

Chapter 5

The Division of Political Power: Ancient Rome

> If a man were called to fix the period in the history of the world during which the condition of the human race was the most happy and prosperous, he would, without hesitation, name that which elapsed from the death of Domitian to the accession of Commodus.[1]

In his 1776 book, *The Decline and Fall of the Roman Empire,* historian Edward Gibbon wrote the best time to live would be as a Roman citizen in 90-180 A.D. Some historians think Gibbon had too much nostalgia for the period. However, the size, wealth, and infrastructure of the Roman Empire during this period was not repeated until modern times.

Gibbon wrote his magisterial history before the American Revolution using the terms "most happy" and "most prosperous." These terms describe the cultural and economic goals of sovereign individuals. In an integral society, the role of government is a referee to prevent and resolve conflict and harm in the cultural and economic spheres. In a civilized society, people have a right to pursue life, liberty, and property so long as those pursuits do not impinge on the rights of others. Government power is needed to referee these pursuits when people commit fouls. But who will referee the government?

---

1.   Edward Gibbon, *The Decline and Fall of the Roman Empire,* abridged by D. M. Low (New York: Harcourt, Brace, 1960), p. 1.

WHO GUARDS THE GUARDIANS?

Who will guard the guardians? This famous question dates back to Plato's *Republic*. In a dialogue, Glaucon asked this question, and Socrates stated that rulers had the moral obligation to act impeccably. Knowledge, virtue, and skill are necessary qualities of leadership. The poet Juvenal asked this question again satirically at the end of the first-century AD[2] after decades of corrupt Emperors in Rome.

Gibbon called this period of peace and stability the rule of "the Five Good Emperors." These were Nerva (reigned 96–98), Trajan (98–117), Hadrian (117–138), Antoninus Pius (138–161), and Marcus Aurelius (161–180).[3] Perhaps they were a social response to Juvenal's message. The five good emperors practiced Stoicism. These philosophies emphasized the perfection of character, personal responsibility, training, hard work, neutrality, and personal sacrifice. These are ideal qualities of good leaders.

Another feature of this period was that transfer of power was not dynastic but to "adopted sons," who were like trained emperor apprentices and not biological heirs. Transfer of political power to family members through inheritance rather than skill and training usually leads to regime failure. Family businesses and other social institutions also suffer from inheritance unless the family member is well-trained and prepared.

The great revival of the Roman Empire did not last beyond these emperors. Marcus Aurelius named his biological son Commodus as his successor. Commodus was insecure, narcissistic, and lacked the skills of his father. Abuse of power and the irresponsible use of power returned to plague the Empire. But the Empire continued despite poor emperors. One reason for its resilience was the distribution of power between the Emperor and the Senate.

---

2. *Quis custodiet ipsos custodes?* A Latin phrase from the Roman poet Juvenal (circa. late first century to early second century A.D.) from his Satires (Satire VI, lines 347–348).

3. "Five Good Emperors," *Encyclopedia Brittanica.* https://www.britannica.com/topic/Five-Good-Emperors.

Today the phrase, "power corrupts, and absolute power corrupts absolutely," has become an axiom.[4] The key message in this axiom is that power should be divided so that checks and balances curtail the abuse of power while allowing its good use to prevail. The Roman Emperors had escaped some checks initially built into the Roman system of governance. Rome originally expanded and prospered because the governance power was divided. Power rested on a social contract between the wealthy elites and the working-class people. I call this form of governance "Life, Liberty, and the Pursuit of Happiness, Version 2.0."[5]

THE SENATE: SEPARATION OF LEGISLATIVE AND EXECUTIVE POWER

The Roman system of governance began as a federation of tribes with a king appointed by the clans' elders. The first king, Romulus, organized a Senate in 753. B.C. The Senate was composed of 100 leaders from among the clans. It served as a council that advised the king, passed laws, and chose future kings. This arrangement divided political power so that no individual held absolute power.

Early Rome experienced power struggles between kings and senators. There were palace intrigues when the kings were leading armies in neighboring lands. Corruption was always a threat. Lucius Tarquinius Superbus, Rome's seventh king, abused his power, put many Senators to death, and caused his wife's suicide. He was driven out of Rome. His nephew, Lucius Junius Brutus, was given the title of 1st Consul and some credit for the founding of the Roman Republic in 509 B.C.

The Republic was more democratic. Two consuls were elected annually. Under emergency situations, they would elect a dictator, but he could not serve more than six months.[6] The Senate wielded much power,

---

4. Lord Action, "Letter to Bishop Creighton," 1887. Famously quoted.

5. Gordon L. Anderson, *Life, Liberty, and the Pursuit of Happiness,* Version 4.0, (St. Paul, MN: Paragon House, 2009), pp. 7-10.

6. "Roman Republic," *Encyclopaedia Britannica* https://www.britannica.com/place/Roman-Republic.

representing the landed wealth and called *patricians*. The Senate made the laws.

TRIBUNES AND POLITICAL EQUALITY AMONG CITIZENS

As Rome prospered, it's population grew, and many people migrated to Rome looking for work. The working people, the *plebs*, who produced goods and served in the military, felt increasingly exploited by the Senate's laws that favored the patricians. This growing populace became tired of working for the elites without representation.

In 494 B.C., the plebs staged a general strike, many leaving the city. The patricians quickly realized how dependent they were on the plebs when they negotiated an agreement for representation in the government. The plebs were allowed to create a council, and elect two representatives, tribunes, to attend Senate meetings. This number later became ten. The plebs could recommend and veto legislation. Patricians were forbidden from laying a hand on plebs, causing bodily harm, a legal recognition that all citizens had sovereignty.

The plebs insisted on writing the laws into a code. This code, the *Twelve Tables,* was produced by 10 appointed commissioners. The commissioners consulted Greek laws and drafted a code that both the plebs and patricians approved. The Twelve Tables were like a constitution describing a system of governance that included the distribution of power, rights, property ownership, and judicial procedures. They were not imposed by a ruler but adopted by a consensus of the governed after research and collaboration.

Over time, the plebeian class became more powerful and fully integrated into Roman society. In 287 B.C. class division between patricians and plebs, known as the Conflict of the Orders, officially ended. The tribes were reclassified to include members of both classes, giving plebs equal power. The governing class was no longer defined by birth, but wealth and achievement. Political equality and sovereignty existed for all Roman citizens. By 172 B.C. plebs had held both consulships.[7]

---

7. Donald L. Wasson, "Plebeians," *World History Encyclopedia*. https://www.world-history.org/Plebeians/.

Democratic power, without traditional checks and balances, became self-destructive in the late Roman Republic. Popular tribunes were elected, making promises to the poor, and then used veto power on any legislation opposed to their policies. Tiberius Sempronius Gracchus (c. 163-133 B.C.) and his brother Gaius Sempronius Gracchus (c. 158-121 B.C.) enacted land reform that transferred land from the wealthy to the poor and gave citizenship to their allies.[8] They were born from an aristocratic family and hijacked the original purpose of the tribunes to represent the working class, combining the wealthy elites outside the aristocracy with a large number of votes of the poor. This institutional hijacking led to civil wars.

The dictator L. Cornelius Sulla stripped tribunes of all legislative power in 80 B.C. The tribunes were restored after Sulla, but the end of the Republic was near. After his defeat of Mark Antony in 31 B.C., Augustus was awarded all the powers of the tribunes in addition to the governing authority of the consulate, becoming the first Emperor of Rome.

DECLINE AND FALL OF THE ROMAN EMPIRE

The initial division of power and the sovereignty of citizens in the Roman Republic enabled the creation of an empire that surpassed the breadth, power, and resilience of the Babylonian Empire. The separation of political power allowed the rise of new cultural and economic institutions. These new social institutions were not significantly checked or refereed.

The consolidation of power, the debasement of the currency, a welfare system, the loss of sovereignty by citizens, and a monopoly on truth contributed to the empire's decline. The collapse of the Roman Empire began with the reign of Marcus Aurelius' son Commodus (180-192). Commodus' rule is an example of the dangers of passing political rule on to children unprepared to rule. Commodus was insecure and lacked his father's leadership skills. He adopted an increasingly dictatorial style of leadership combined with the psychological need to justify his worthiness, culminating in his performance as a gladiator in the Colosseum.

---

8. "Gaius Gracchus," *Encyclopedia Brittanica,* https://www.britannica.com/biography/Gaius-Sempronius-Gracchus

Many historians blame the fall on invasions from the outside. But these invasions were possible because of the decay of the empire from within. Power became bureaucratized, centralized, and corrupt. Welfare programs initiated to quell unrest became entitlement programs too large to finance. The economic sovereignty of the middle classes was destroyed by the debasement of money, taxes, and the appropriation of their property.

ROMAN WELFARE, IMPORTED SLAVES, AND DEPENDENCY

Food subsidies and entitlements began in the late years of the Roman Republic and expanded during the period of the empire. Poorer citizens of Rome became desperate for food when prices increased due to supply chain disruptions and war.

Gaius Gracchus (158-122 B.C.) proposed that the government procure an adequate supply of wheat to be sold at a fixed price, about half the market price, to everyone willing to stand in line for a monthly allotment.[9] Then a politician named Clodius ran for tribune on a free wheat platform and won. When Julius Caesar (c. 100-44 B.C.) came to power a decade later, there were over 320,000 people on the grain relief program.[10]

It was too politically unpopular to stop the grain programs, like modern social security and entitlement programs. They continued for centuries with over 200,000 recipients.[11] Free grain was a burden on state finances, and it reduced the incentive of people to work in productive enterprises or serve in the military—things needed for the empire to be secure and prosper.

Another problem was the economic impact on the slaves arriving from conquering foreign lands. This cheap labor displaced many

9. H.J. Haskell, *The New Deal in Ancient Rome* (New York: A.A. Knopf, 1939), p. 110.

10. Ibid., p. 113.

11. M, Rostovtzeff, *The Social and Economic History of the Roman Empire* (Oxford: Clarendon Press, second edition, 1957), pp. 81-2.

working-class wage-earners, who then qualified for free grain and other handouts. The free grain caused a dependency on the government and undermined the traditional Roman virtue of self-reliance.[12]

CURRENCY DEBASEMENT, DISEASE, TAXES, AND FEUDALISM

Currency debasement aided the collapse of Rome and the rise of feudalism. Currency debasement causes similar economic injustices as central banks creating fiat money today. Modern money debasement comes from fractional reserve debt creation and overprinting of money. Rome's currency debasement was minting new coins with reduced silver content. The content of silver in coins was over 95 percent in 64 A.D. This declined to less than 5 percent by 265 A.D.[13] The inflationary effects were a hidden tax on the citizens. The amount of money in the economy no longer represented the value of goods and services. It took more coins to buy a house or a shop.

When the emperors spent the new currency, it entered the economy through government expenditures to expand the bureaucracy and pay for military exploits. The military and political classes gained more money and purchasing power than the hard-working middle classes. Currency debasement was a hidden tax. But direct taxes on citizens increased.

During Marcus Aurelius' reign, a plague of smallpox broke out. At its peak in 189 A.D. 2,000 people in Rome died daily. Ten percent of the 75 million people in the empire never recovered. Many of the aristocracy, military, and council members died and were replaced with less-skilled people, immigrants, and sons of slaves.[14] Marcus Aurelius settled a large number of foreigners on Roman soil. Rome survived, and Gibbon did not mention this disease as a reason for the empire's fall. Yet, it impacted

---

12. Henry Hazlitt, "Poor Relief in Ancient Rome," Foundation for Economic Education. https://fee.org/articles/poor-relief-in-ancient-rome/.

13. Jeff Desjardins, "Currency and the Collapse of the Roman Empire," *Visual Capitalist*, https://www.visualcapitalist.com/currency-and-the-collapse-of-the-roman-empire/

14. Edward Watts, "What Rome Learned From the Deadly Antonine Plague of 165 A.D." *Smithsonian Magazine*, April 28, 2020. https://www.smithsonianmag.com/history/what-rome-learned-deadly-antonine-plague-165-d-180974758/.

the leadership, who would be less skilled and less invested in the success of the empire.

Taxes increased, and state demands destroyed entrepreneurs and businesses. H.J. Haskell wrote:

> Heavy contributions of grain were exacted from farmers to feed the soldiers and the population of the large cities. There were land taxes, property taxes, occupation taxes, poll taxes. It has been said of this period that "the penalty of wealth seemed to be ruin." The heart was taken out of the enterprising men. Finally the burden became so intolerable that to escape the Imperial levies tenants fled from the farms and business men and workmen from their occupations. The government intervened and bound the tenants to the soil—the beginning of serfdom—and the business men and workmen to their occupations and trades. Private enterprise was crushed and the state was forced to take over many kinds of business to keep the machine running.[15]

Julius Caesar changed Roman law to allow bankers to confiscate land in lieu of loan payments.[16] Before this, the land was untouchable, and debts would be passed to descendants.[17] The legal seizure of assets and high inflation caused middle-class citizens to lose businesses and farms to wealthy elites. The military leaders and government officials who had acquired the debased money could buy the foreclosed properties and become feudal lords. The descendants of a once-vibrant Roman middle class became serfs, sometimes on land their parents had owned.

Diocletian (r. 284-305) moved the seat of government from the city of Rome to Nicomedia, near modern Istanbul. As the Western Empire collapsed, Germans filled the ruined provinces and lived alongside the native populace. "The Romans grew more barbarized. The Germans became more civilized."[18] In 476, the last emperor of the Roman line,

---

15. H.J. Haskell, *The New Deal in Ancient Rome*, op. cit., p. 221.

16. Andrew Beattie, "The Evolution of Banking," *Forbes*, https://www.forbes.com/sites/investopedia/2011/11/03/the-evolution-of-banking/

17. Andrew Beattie, "The Evolution of Banking Over Time," *Investopedia*, https://www.investopedia.com/articles/07/banking.asp.

18. Quote from J.W. Thompson in Haskell, *op. cit.*, p. 222.

Romulus Augustulus, was told to resign, and there was no longer an emperor in the West. The city of Rome was never again the political capital of the empire.

Feudalism arose with the disappearance of the middle class and a loss of individual economic sovereignty. When the government has the power of monopoly on money, and the ownership of wealth is in the hands of a few, common citizens are deprived of equal opportunity for economic advancement. Those who lobbied or served the government became wealthy, while those who produced the goods and services necessary for life became poor.

THE ESTABLISHMENT OF RELIGION AND THE DARK AGES

Gibbon argued that the establishment of Christianity was the reason for Rome's decline, saying it created weak citizens reluctant to fight an enemy. But, Rome was already crumbling before the rise of Christianity because the vibrant middle class lost its sovereignty. Citizens are unwilling to fight when they are not defending their property. They would fight to protect their own land and pursue their own dreams, but they are not happy to support other people's wars or dreams. The new populations of Germans and Huns had little commitment to Rome. The more significant problem was the loss of loyalty to a regime that had destroyed personal sovereignty.

Constantine sought another way to get loyal and virtuous citizens. He gave Christianity legal status to stem moral relativism and loss of obedience to the regime. The Church had become a more admired and trusted social institution. Christians honored the Ten Commandments, were known as honest citizens, and "rendered the Caesar that which was Caesar's."

Constantine convened the Council of Nicaea (325 A.D.) to establish official Church doctrine. Theodosius I, in 380 A.D., declared Christianity as the only legitimate imperial religion. He ended state support for the traditional Roman religion, giving Christianity a monopoly on truth. Zealous followers of Theodosius I, anxious to wipe out the vestiges of paganism, likely destroyed what was left of the Library of Alexandria and much ancient knowledge.[19] Dogmatists censored secular knowledge and science and burned unorthodox books.

The Church used its monopoly for indoctrination and thought control. Individuals became believers rather than truth seekers. They were told salvation depended on their obedience to the church. Individuals lost cultural sovereignty.

CONCLUSION

The distribution of political power in Ancient Rome laid the foundation for one of the greatest civilizations to arise. It began as a federation of tribes represented by Senators who appointed executive leaders. The working class next got representation and eventually full citizenship and equality. At its peak in the second-century A.D., the city of Rome had a population of up to 2 million people. Roman citizenship meant freedom and personal sovereignty.

The Roman system eventually collapsed from problems the governance structure created or did not address. First of all, the late Republic collapsed when popular Tribunes overstepped their purpose of representing the interests of the working class and instead pandered to coalitions of wealthy elites and the poor and against the traditional system of governance. Pandering led to civil war and the rise of emperors with more concentrated power.

Internal cultural and economic weaknesses were caused by corrupt family dynasties, expensive military exploits, the debasement of money, unbearable taxes, and the destruction of the productive middle class and the citizens' self-reliance. An empire of sovereign citizens with the opportunity for upward economic mobility degenerated into warring states whose masses had become serfs with no personal sovereignty or the possibility of upward economic mobility.

---

19. Mostafa El-Abbadi, "Library of Alexandria," *Encyclopedia Brittanica.* https://www.britannica.com/topic/Library-of-Alexandria/The-fate-of-the-Library-of-Alexandria. Much of the library was lost during a war in 48 B.C., when Julius Caesar set fire to enemy ships and the fire spread to the city.

The fourth-century attempt to establish the Church as the official source of truth deprived individuals of their cultural sovereignty. By 550 A.D. the population of the city of Rome had declined to about 30,000 people, governed by the Pope.[20]

Some historians say the empire's decline was because of its population loss. It was the reverse; Rome's population declined because political, economic, and cultural sovereignty was lost. The policies to support the population through welfare and higher taxes caused a downward spiral. During the rise of Rome, there were great opportunities for upward economic and social mobility, even for immigrants and slaves. Hard work was a path to citizenship. The decline of Rome followed the loss of individual sovereignty as the middle classes experienced downward social mobility and eventually serfdom.

The Dark Ages had arrived. Most people earned and owned little and had little opportunity to pursue happiness. The path of hope for a better life had changed from hard work, personal responsibility, and ingenuity to cunning and intrigue. People's only hope was a fairy tale, marry the handsome prince or beautiful princess. Individual sovereignty was gone.

---

20. Kevin Twine, "The City In Decline: Rome In Late Antiquity," *Middle States Geographer*, Vol. 25, 1992, pp. 134-138.

Chapter
6

From Feudalism to Modern Individual Sovereignty

The Dark Ages began with the institutional monopolies of the Church and State, reinforcing one another. They were the source of power, money, and truth. Most were the pawns of these institutions and lived subsistence lives at their mercy. Feudalism was not a return to tribal hunter-gatherer society or life under kings or tyrants, but life under the control of monopolistic institutions without checks and balances on power.

Institutions had claimed sovereignty. Individuals who flourished as sovereigns in Rome with the opportunity to pursue happiness disappeared along with the powerful empire they had produced. Ending the Dark Ages required removing these monopolies and restoring individual sovereignty.

THE SEPARATION OF TWO SOCIAL SPHERES

The separation of two social spheres, culture and governance, can be viewed as an evolutionary advance in human society, even though the monopolies in those spheres were not. The longer goal of social evolution would be to split into three social spheres, with checks and balances on institutions in each of these spheres that support individual rights and self-responsibility.

The Dark Ages were characterized by a struggle between the Church and the State. How should the sovereigns of each sphere, the emperors and the popes, relate to one another? Which sphere is responsible for what? This was the primary social question for feudal society. The Eastern and Western halves of the Old Roman Empire answered this question differently. In the East, which lasted until the fall of Constantinople in 1453, the Church remained subservient to the Emperor. In the West, which fell to the Ostrogoths in 476 A.D., the Church gained more influence as political power fragmented into small and mid-size states.

Economically, the Church was independent of the kings. It owned significant property and was a feudal landholder, with economic income from monasteries and farms. The Church had soldiers to defend its properties, giving it enough temporal power to assist powerful kings and coerce less powerful ones.

THE RISE OF THE POWER OF THE CHURCH

Popes were initially elected by bishops and approved by church members, but after Christianity became the official religion of the Empire, emperors claimed the authority to approve popes. Sometimes emperors bribed bishops to get the popes they wanted to be elected.

The Ostrogoth Kings in the West (493-537) wanted to approve a Pope, but otherwise interfered little with the affairs of the Church. The Church controlled the city of Rome and other properties throughout the West. Justinian I, the Eastern Emperor, acquired Rome, creating a Byzantine Papacy (537-752). He required the approval or selection of popes for consecration by the Emperor.

The Popes eventually broke Rome away from the East and allied with kings in the West. In 800 A.D., Pope Leo III crowned Charlemagne, King of the Franks and Lombards, as Roman Emperor. The Church obtained the protection of the Western Emperor and culturally asserted itself over the Emperor. This alliance began the Holy Roman Empire, although the term was not used until the 13th century.

The Holy Roman Empire was not a unitary state but a loose federation of Christian States. An Imperial College elected the Holy Roman Emperor. The papal election decree (1059) of Nicholas II removed kings from the process of electing popes. Pope Gregory VII (1076) reorganized the structure of Church institutions to be independent of secular rulers and reduce the role of the laity in ecclesiastical affairs. The Popes now had control of the culture with no checks and balances on their power.

THE CRUSADES AND THE ABUSE OF CHURCH POWER

After the Norman Conquest of England in 1066, Western Europe regained the military capacity to launch the Crusades. The ability to direct political rulers emboldened popes to call for Holy Wars. Pope Urban II called for the First Crusade (1095) under the banner of the "Peace of God," a movement to limit warfare to defend clergy, travelers, women, cattle, and others unable to protect themselves from robbers and gangs. Christians retook Jerusalem after over 400 years under Muslim rule.

The Church used crusades and pogroms to stomp out heretical churches, Jews, and free thinkers. The massacre at Béziers in July 1209 represents the evils that can be done when military power enforces official truth. When soldiers invaded the town and discovered there were both loyal Catholics and heretical Cathari, they reportedly asked the abbot what to do. The abbot, citing 2 Timothy 2:19, declared, "Kill them all for the Lord knoweth them that are His." And so, countless numbers of both Catholics and heretics were slain in the name of God.[1]

The Church in the Middles Ages incentivized fighters to engage in a religious war, much as Muslim jihadists are promised glory in heaven. Many crusaders believed that a "crusade indulgence" officially absolved all their previous sins and ensured salvation in the afterlife.

With increased power, the Church experienced more corruption. Wealth and power influenced the selection of popes and their policies. The buying or selling of ecclesiastical privileges was known as *simony*. Popes and priests sold pardons to wealthy people they had excommunicated.

---

1. *Medieval Sourcebook: Caesarius of Heisterbach: Medieval Heresies*, Chapter XXI. Fordham University. https://sourcebooks.fordham.edu/source/caesarius-heresies.asp.

They sold sacred objects for private gain. And they sold administrative offices.

The Church concentrated its control on truth, salvation, and wealth as political authority decentralized in the late medieval and early modern periods. Power began to shift from agricultural lords to commercial centers.

COMMERCE AND THE DECLINE OF FEUDAL POWER

The maritime cities of Venice, Genoa, and Pisa first built up autonomy as centers of trade. As imperial authority retreated from Italy, the natural pursuit of economic sovereignty stimulated the Renaissance in Florence and Milan. Money was injected into society through banks for businesses and private houses in cities that grew in wealth. People in the North sought economic freedom, and *burghers* (mayors) pressed feudal lords for concessions that allowed for urbanization.

These freedoms allowed natural social organizations to emerge. In the towns, artisans organized into guilds that soon garnered political influence and controlled production, labor markets, and tariffs.[2] The cities created alliances with the Hanseatic League in Germany and the Lombard League in Northern Italy.

Urbanization enabled the rise of a new commercial middle-class. Between 1000 and 1200, the urban population doubled or tripled. The production and trade of food, clothing, military tools, and household goods expanded the economies of cities and enabled the arts to flourish.

Modern universities began as schools to teach international students the liberal arts, law, and theology. The University of Bologna began in 1088 and was given a charter by Emperor Frederick I Barbarossa in 1158. Universities taught philosophy, medicine, logic, theology, law, mathematics, astronomy, and grammar. Their graduates served as leaders in the growing commercial civilization, and the institutions brought revenue from students and prestige to cities.

2. Simon Duits, "Holy Roman Empire," *World History Encyclopedia.* https://www.worldhistory.org/Holy_Roman_Empire/.

The Church prospered from these developments and built large cathedrals and monasteries in the cities. St. Peter's Basilica in Rome flaunted ornate renaissance design. The decentralization of political power, the rise of cities, economic development, and the founding of universities did not initially challenge the monopoly on moral authority by the Church, which considered this the flowering of its Christian empire.

LITERACY AND THE PROTESTANT REFORMATION

The movable-type printing press, a technological invention, did more to undermine the monopoly of the Church on knowledge than the Protestant Reformers who soon followed. The Gutenberg Bible was printed in Mainz, Germany, in 1455 by Johann Gutenberg and his associates, Johann Fust and Peter Schoeffer. It was a version of the Latin Vulgate, the Bible used by Catholic clergy since St. Jerome compiled it in 387. This was not new or controversial knowledge, but it became available to everyone, and people could buy books and have them in their homes.

Books were previously handwritten and kept in the Church's and universities' libraries. The publication of the Gutenberg Bible and other books meant that people could read and study for themselves without relying on the oral teachings of the clergy or professors. Literacy in Europe quickly grew as books became available.

The Bible contained many books in the Old Testament known to the Jews but rarely taught by the Church. Individuals could compare what they read to what the Church taught and did. Readers could distinguish biblical truth from Church propaganda and compare the lives of church leaders with that taught by Jesus. Reading was a vehicle for individual cultural sovereignty that the Church could not control.

Martin Luther, and Augustinian monk, was the spearhead of the Protestant Reformation. Augustine (340–430) had emphasized the primacy of the Bible rather than Church teaching as the ultimate religious authority. A serious and conscientious scholar, he traveled to Rome and witnessed extravagances spent by the Church on itself, like St. Peter's Basilica. These expenses were funded by indulgences, a scheme the Church used to extract money from believers with promises of salvation. Luther believed salvation came from personal faith in God and the Church abused poor Germans.

In 1517, Luther posted his "Disputation on the Power and Efficacy of Indulgences" on the door of the Wittenburg Castle church, offering to debate the topic. The Church was not interested in debate but in suppressing ideas that challenged its authority, power, or wealth. Accused of heresy, Luther refused to recant at the Diet of Worms (1521). He was taken prisoner for his safety by Frederick, elector of Saxony, and held for nearly a year in Wartburg Castle. There he began the translation of the New Testament into German, significantly developing the German language and, indirectly, the emergence of other national languages.

Luther was not as radical as many later reformers, but he represented the end of the Church's cultural monopoly. The Protestant Reformation led to religious pluralism in Europe. Princes and Kings chose which religion would be the official religion of their states. Brutal religious wars raged following the Protestant Reformation until the Peace of Westphalia (1648), when the Spanish Empire lost control of the Netherlands. The modern state system was created in Europe. The Netherlands became the first state to allow the freedom of religion.

INDIVIDUAL SOVEREIGNTY AND THE RISE OF DEMOCRACY

Protestantism introduced the idea of personal sovereignty: each person is responsible for their life on earth and ultimately accountable to God. The Protestant consciousness is a self-driven individual. One does not wait for instructions from a feudal master or a priest but studies and prays to do what is right. Protestant consciousness has much in common with stoicism, an internal striving for virtue and perfection. That philosophy guided the five good emperors of ancient Rome. Protestant culture promoted self-perfection, hard work, and passing these values on to the next generation.

Protestantism cultivated the type of people who were capable of self-rule and minimal government. The Ten Commandments passed down from ancient civilizations through the Bible promoted civil behavior.

Modern social theorists shared these fundamental cultural values and, freed from the constraints of religious dogma, developed rational and critical thought seeking to understand universal laws and the principles of nature. René Descartes (1596–1650), the founder of modern philosophy and critical thought, began with the premise *cogito ergo sum,* "I think, therefore I am."[3] This philosophy supports individual cultural sovereignty is supported by this philosophy.

In his *Second Treatise on Government,* one of the most influential social theorists, John Locke (1632-1704),[4] rationally concluded that individual sovereignty requires the right to life, liberty, and property. The government's duty is to secure these rights:

> Every Man has a Property in his own Person. This no Body has any Right to but himself. The Labour of his Body, and the Work of his Hands, we may say, are properly his.[5]

Jean Jacques Rousseau (1712-1778)[6] sought to find a way of preserving human freedom in a world where human beings are increasingly interdependent. In *The Social Contract,* he explored constructing political institutions that allow for the co-existence of free and equal citizens in a community where they are individually sovereign.

These philosophers, in addition to Thomas Hobbes, Montesquieu, Adam Smith, and David Hume contributed ideas to shape a constitution for a republican form of democracy in which power rested in a consensus of the governed. New republican political institutions that enabled democratic self-rule while checking the abuse of power were necessary and becoming possible.

---

3. Rene Descarte, *Discourse on Method,* 1637.

4. "John Locke," *Stanford Encyclopedia of Philosophy.* https://plato.stanford.edu/entries/locke/.

5. John Locke, "Second Treatise," in *Two Treatises of Government,* ed. Peter Laslett (Cambridge: Cambridge University Press, 1988), Sec. 27.

6. "Jean Jacques Rousseau," *Stanford Encyclopedia of Philosophy.* https://plato.stanford.edu/entries/rousseau/

Chapter

7

Individual Sovereignty and the U.S. Founding

INDIVIDUAL SOVEREIGNTY: THE BASIS OF INTEGRAL SOCIETY

Individual sovereignty is more than the unity of mind and body. The sovereign individual's internal and external aspects transcend control of the physical body and include knowledge, productivity, and behavior. These are the individual components of the three culture spheres. Individual sovereignty is represented by the upper two quadrants in Wilber's integral framework. Social institutions require sovereign individuals to function.

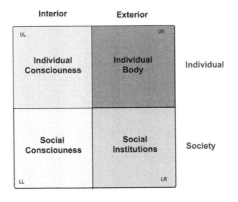

Figure 1: Individual Sovereignty and Social Institutions in Four Quadrants (see Appendix)

Individual sovereignty is a prerequisite for an integral society. Individual sovereignty requires the right to life, liberty, and property; it includes the mastery of life, liberty, and property, but that does not make one sovereign. A sovereign individual assumes responsibility for economic sufficiency, self-governance, and the pursuit of happiness. Rights and responsibilities are both necessary.

Integral society begins with sovereign individuals who have an integral social consciousness. Their consciousness transcends the self, respects the rights of others, and understands the role of social institutions in a complex society. In the last chapter, we discuss the background of the evolution of individual sovereignty in the cultural, economic, and political spheres as the West emerged from feudalism. The process began in the cultural sphere with the Renaissance, literacy, and the Reformation.

A culture of personal responsibility increased production and commerce, and less-centralized government in Europe provided new opportunities for individuals to pursue happiness. This cultural evolution stimulated a widespread desire of people to be in charge of their political and economic life, not relying on the dictates of kings and popes.

Individual Sovereignty at the U.S. Founding

The Colonies in North America provided new economic opportunities for those individuals willing to leave Europe behind and create a new life for themselves. In the North, individuals and families ran their farms and businesses and organized community institutions that needed little governance.

Although few Americans had an integral level of consciousness at the founding, most were sovereign individuals. They were economically independent and voluntarily chose to live in colonies with similar cultural values. Wealthy aristocrats and slaves comprised only about 25 percent of the population in 1790, many of whom were in the South. The majority of self-reliant people paralleled the Roman population when the Twelve Tables were adopted.

Individual sovereignty means self-ownership. Individual sovereignty is a better way to describe the foundation for an integral society than middle-class incomes, although there is a strong correlation between the two. The U.S. Constitution is a system of governance created for people of individual sovereignty, and when the U.S. was founded, such a population existed in the North.

POLITICAL PHILOSOPHY AT THE U.S. FOUNDING

The U.S. Founders used the latest political theories and the lessons of ancient Greece and Rome to create a "more perfect union" in the U.S. Constitution. The goal of the Constitution was a governance system to serve the mission stated in The United States Declaration of Independence (1776), "Life, Liberty, and the Pursuit of Happiness." John Locke's formulation of "life, liberty, and property" was clearly stated in the 5th Amendment to the U.S. Constitution:

> ...nor shall any person ... be deprived of life, liberty, or property, without due process of law; nor shall private property be taken for public use, without just compensation.[1]

The founders read Hobbes, Locke, Hume, Rousseau, Gibbon's history of the decline of the Roman Empire, Adam Smith's economic theory, and Montesquieu's work on the separation of powers in government. They knew the British government's strengths and problems of corruption from first-hand experience. A primary goal was to prevent moneyed interests or religious groups from taking political power from the citizens.

Ken Wilber stated that several of the Founders had reached an integral or "second-tier consciousness."[2] They could think holistically and integrate the highest levels of first-tier consciousness to develop a system of state governance based on individual sovereignty.

The Constitution enshrined the right to life, liberty, and property. It divided power between the people, the states, and seasoned leadership. It provided checks and balances and new legislation with a consensus of the people's representatives in Congress and a consensus of the states'

---

1. U.S. Constitution, Amendment 5, Section 1
2. Ken Wilber, *A Theory of Everything,* pp. 13-16, 89-90.

representatives in the Senate.[3] At the end of the 18th century, only a tiny percentage of the population had reached the level of consciousness necessary to sustain the Republic.[4] People would need an elevated moral consciousness to "keep the Republic."[5]

Economic Democracy at the U.S. Founding

The majority of U.S. citizens were sovereign economically at the founding. Life for this group of people could be considered economic democracy. People were farmers, tradesmen, or businessmen who owned the fruits of their own labor. Economist Louis O. Kelso (1913-91) considered the state of nature to be an "economic democracy" because each person has one "labor power."[6] At the founding of the United States, 95 percent of economic production was based on such labor power.[7]

Therefore, the U.S. founders introduced their republican form of political democracy into an existing economic democracy. Economic democracy existed as a prerequisite to self-rule. Giving everyone equal access to resources has not been as easy as giving each person a vote.[8] The land frontier offered a safety valve that provided everyone an opportunity

---

3. The 17th Amendment, which ended state appointment of Senators, terminated this important check on "mob mentality" of the people by enabling people to appoint both representatives and Senators. It violated the spirit of the founding, essentially removing states from representation in their own union.

4. Wilber believed about 20 percent of the population was at the red level and perhaps 40 percent at the blue, ibid., pp. 9-10.

5. One story has Benjamin Franklin telling a woman, "we have given you a Republic if you can keep it." Franklin also reportedly told his daughter that she needed spiritual nourishment every week, but she could attend any church or synagogue.

6. Louis O. Kelso interview by Harold Channer. https://www.youtube.com/watch?v=lRPT3SFkndA.

7. Ibid.

8. Having a vote does not guarantee equal access to power if moneyed interests, political parties, and other lobbyists intervene. The U.S. founders created governance structures that allowed legislation only by the consent of the governed. However, these structures were eventually eroded by parties and interests and today deny sovereign individuals equal access to political power.

to be self-sufficient.[9] If one did not own a business or have a marketable skill, one could obtain land and grow food to feed oneself. In a society based on labor power and not a capitalist system, the basic economic laws of Adam Smith in *The Wealth of Nations* (1776) applied.[10]

With economic sovereignty, democracy in America was possible, as Alexis de Tocqueville laid out in his 1835 book *Democracy in America*.[11] Aristotle made this point in his *Politics*:

> An agricultural population makes the best demos; so that it is possible to make a democracy anywhere where the population subsists on agriculture or stock-raising and pastures... They do not lack the necessities. So they do not covet others possessions. They find more satisfaction in working the land than in the duties of government... [12]

Thomas Jefferson firmly believed in this, writing to James Madison:

> I think our governments will remain virtuous for many centuries; as long as they are chiefly agricultural; and this will be as long as there are vacant lands in any part of America. When they get piled upon one another in large cities as in Europe, they will become corrupt as in Europe.[13]

Jefferson's 530 million acres Louisiana Purchase in 1803 extended the land available for immigrating farmers by decades. By 1893, when Frederick Jackson Turner published his frontier thesis,[14] the vacant lands were largely filled, and people began "piling upon one another in large cities as in Europe."

---

9. See, Frederick Jackson Turner, "The Significance of the Frontier in American History," 1893.

10. Adam Smith, *The Wealth of Nations,* ed. Andrew Skinner (NY: Penguin Books, 1970).

11. Alexis de Tocqueville, *Democracy in America,* abridged and edited by Richard D. Heffner, New York: New American Library, 1956.

12. Aristotle, *The Politics,* trans. and ed. T.A. Sinclair (NY: Penguin Classic, 1962), Book VI, Chapter 4.

13. Thomas Jefferson, "Letter to James Madison, 20 December, 1787," *The Papers of Thomas Jefferson,* ed. Julian P. Boyd (Princeton University Press, 1958), vol. 12, p. 442.

14. Frederick Jackson Turner, "The Significance of the Frontier in American History," *op. cit.*.

As available land disappeared, a new industrial frontier was arising. This provided economic opportunities in producing new types of goods and services designed with the help of science, technology, capital, and machines. The industrial frontier made widespread individual economic sovereignty possible after the agricultural frontier was exhausted.

Industrialization in the twentieth century stimulated the growth of economic social institutions like banking, stock trading, and globalization, which eventually usurped individual economic self-sufficiency. Economic injustices as in Europe that gave power to the Marxist critique of the class system of wealth. Part 3 analyzes inadequately regulated money and banking, the Marxist critique of the current economic system, and alternatives for economic sovereignty.

CONCLUSION

Part 2 of this book is a brief survey of the evolution of society from tribal societies to highly populated societies with complex social institutions. It has emphasized the following points:

1. An integral society develops from the innate desire of individuals to communicate, exchange goods and services, have families, and pursue happiness.

2. An integral society requires sustainable production of goods and services rather than theft from nature or other people.

3. Integral society is developed with an integral consciousness in which social institutions serve individual citizens.

4. A Republican form of democracy requires a large middle class, in which citizens have economic autonomy.

5. Social institutions fall into three social spheres: culture, economy, and governance. These social spheres are grounded in different social principles.

6. Integral society involves a reversal of rule from the top-down

imposition of power to a bottom-up consensus of sovereign citizens.

7. Civilizations have risen and fallen based on the degree to which they have created and supported sovereign individuals.

Part 3 examines possibilities for transforming current societies into more integral ones. Changes in social institutions in all three social spheres are required, but a focus on the economic sphere and its entanglement with governance is most critical.

Historical evolution has never developed an honest fractional reserve banking system or adequately separated the creation of money from government control. History provides a blueprint for cultural and political sovereignty, which developed after feudal society. However, modern capitalism has not been properly instituted or regulated. Economic sovereignty in the contemporary world means that all individuals should have an equal opportunity to own the fruits of both labor power and capital power.

Part 3

The Transformation of
Social Institutions

Chapter
8

Individual Sovereignty and Institutional Sovereignty

INTRODUCTION

People create institutions to serve their sovereignty, make life better and facilitate the individual pursuit of happiness. But institutions want to rule the world. Since the apex of individual sovereignty in the United States at the turn of the 18th century, social institutions have been on the march to appropriate that sovereignty for themselves.

The State, which should be a referee serving sovereign citizens, has been the primary political institution bent on usurping individual sovereignty. All the major world religions teach that each individual is a child of God, can be the dwelling place of God, or can attain God-consciousness. The primary argument for the sovereignty of the state was advanced by the German philosopher Hegel, who argued:

> The state is absolutely rational inasmuch as it is the actuality of the substantial will which it possesses in the particular self-consciousness once that consciousness has been raised to consciousness of its universality. This substantial unity is an absolute unmoved end in itself, in which freedom comes into its supreme right. On the other hand this final end has supreme right *against the individual,* whose supreme duty is to be a member of the state.[1]

---

1. G.W.F. Hegel, *Philosophy of Right,* Part 3: The Ethical Life, Section iii: The State, No. 258 (New York: Oxford University Press, 1977, p. 155. Italics mine.

Hegel saw the state as the culmination of the Absolute (God) march in history. For him, the state, not the individual, was the source of world salvation. The above passage implies that the state has the right to expunge individuals that do not conform to its consciousness. Marx and other "left-wing Hegelians" used this to justify the state seizure of private property. And one might argue that Hitler justified genocide by the state on the same basis. Dictators and political parties that believe they are justified in using state power to achieve their ends have killed and oppressed millions of individuals they should have served.

Economic corporations, organized to get enough capital to produce large amounts of products for individual consumers, have been taken over by global investors who use them for profit regardless of their effect on consumers. David C. Korten, the founder of the People-centered Development Forum, has written:

> Driven by the single-minded dedication to generating ever greater profits for the benefit of their investors, global corporations and financial institutions have turned their economic power into political power. They now dominate the decision processes of governments and are rewriting the rules of world commerce through international trade and investment agreements to allow themselves to expand their profits without regard to the social and environmental consequences borne by the larger society. Continuing with business as usual will almost certainly lead to economic, social and environmental collapse.[2]

Three large investment firms have significant control of corporations as diverse as Apple, Microsoft, Google, Pfizer, Tesla, Exxon, Berkshire-Hathaway, J.P. Morgan Chase, Home Depot, Proctor and Gamble, United Health, and Amazon. They can use their media holdings to promote their pharmaceutical and technology holdings. They can use social media they control to censor competition. And they can create capital cartels to pool their holdings to put small companies out of business and offshore production to the countries that promise the most profit. They are trying to control the world economy.

---

2. David C. Korten, *The Post-Corporate World: Life After Capitalism* (San Francisco, CA: Berrett-Koehler, 1999), p.6.

BlackRock manages nearly $10 trillion in investments. Vanguard has $8 trillion, and State Street has $4 trillion. Their combined $22 trillion in managed assets is the equivalent of more than half of the combined value of all shares for companies in the S&P 500 (about $38 trillion). Their power is expected to grow. An analysis published in the *Boston University Law Review* in 2019 estimated that the Big Three could control as much as 40 percent of shareholder votes in the S&P 500 within two decades.[3]

Culture is another way institutions try to rule the world. Today, some of the largest economic and political players are trying to promote cultural views like "wokeism" to shape the world for their power and money, masked by slogans of progressivism and justice.

But the woke are engaging in a much larger international arena. One question raised by the woke movement, though hardly ever asked, is whether the U.S. will be able to deploy this new intellectual tool for exporting American cultural influence. Put another way: If there is going to be an international progressive class, why not Americanize it?

Wokeism is an idea that can be adapted to virtually every country: Identify a major form of oppression in a given region or nation, argue that people should be more sensitive to it, add some rhetorical flourishes, purge some wrongdoers (and a few innocents) and voila—you have created another woke movement.

As the technology writer and lawyer Paul Skallas has written: "MeToo and BlackLivesMatter are essentially US culture issues which provide an effective identity for internationals of the progressive class." Almost every other country now has its own version of woke, though it may differ greatly from the American version.[4]

Today's major culture wars are less about differences between conservative and liberal philosophies and more about a contest between the

---

3. Farhad Manjoo, "What BlackRock, Vanguard and State Street Are Doing to the Economy," *New York Times,* May 12, 2022.

4. Tyler, Cowan, "Why Wokeism Will Rule the World," *Bloomberg,* U.S. Edition, September 19, 2021.

sovereignty of institutions and the sovereignty of individuals. Institutions can accumulate more power and wealth than sovereign citizens. They must keep to their mission of serving sovereign citizens rather than being hijacked and used to exploit citizens.

INSTITUTIONAL MISSION

Integral society keeps social institutions in their place. To serve their mission, they must function in the level and sphere of society appropriate to that mission (see Figure 8, Appendix). The most severe dysfunction of social institutions occurring in all spheres and at all levels of society is the failure to remain structured for their mission. Institutions should build incentives to serve their mission in their culture and structure.

Social institutions, whether they are government agencies, corporations, or NGOs, inevitably try to expand beyond the scope of their mission. Leaders are tempted to use institutional resources for other purposes that will enrich themselves. They are tempted to move into other levels and spheres and even exploit their base. Conscientious leaders refuse such temptation.

SOCIAL VIRUSES AND THE HIJACKING OF INSTITUTIONS

One of the clearest examples of institutional hijacking is the misuse of institutional money. Temptations abound when individuals have control of other people's money. Theft can occur in many ways, from the embezzlement by a bookkeeper to leaders spending funds unrelated to the organization's mission. Such theft can happen to any social institution—states, churches, schools, businesses, utilities, hospitals, and charities.

The hijacking of social institutions is analogous to how viruses infect the human body or a computer. The resources meant to serve a specific purpose of the institution, the host, are diverted to serve another purpose of the parasite. The infection will kill or weaken the host without an immune system or anti-virus software that blocks it. Resilient social institutions need both an internal immune system and outside policing. Transparency is one method to hold people in institutions accountable, and secrecy is the most apparent sign of institutional hijacking. Good investigative journalists suspect a crime has been committed when evidence is hidden or documents are classified.

The most consistent areas of institutional abuse involve concentrations of money. Any large pool of money invites theft and misuse. People become motivated to take institutional money rather than use it for its purpose. The Great Depression was caused by the misuse of deposits by banks. Banks overstepped their mission in the 1920s and put individuals at risk by speculating on the stock market with their bank deposits. This was an act of theft. The speculation fueled a stock market bubble that eventually burst, causing many banks to fail from 1930-1933. Many individuals lost their savings.

The Glass-Steagall Act (1933) limited banks to their fundamental mission—banking. The Act forbade banks' use of people's savings for speculative investments and required collateralized loans and enough reserves to guarantee repayment. The Act performed as anti-virus protection.

We have significantly advanced knowledge of the human immune system and anti-virus software. Still, we have not applied similar efforts to create resilient social institutions focused on their mission. Infected social institutions are taking a significant toll on human beings, causing wars, genocides, financial collapses, food shortages, and human trafficking. In all of these social problems, social institutions fail to serve their mission due to hijacking or incompetence. The Glass-Steagall Act is a rare example of the government acting as a good economic referee.

INSTITUTIONAL VALUE TRANSMISSION

The emerging study of Institutional Value Transmission (IVT) and Institutional Resilience[5] by Don Trubshaw and others sheds light on the dysfunction of social institutions. Social institutions are founded for a

---

5. Don Trubshaw,"Institutional Resilience and Ecological Threats as Factors in Societal Peace and Conflict," *International Journal on World Peace,* Vol. XXXVIII, No. 4 (December 2021), pp. 11-37.

purpose and often have a mission statement that generates a set of values and an institutional culture. These values should underpin the core mission of workers, managers, and elites. They serve as a basis for the rules, checks and balances, and other institutional structures that produce the desired product or outcome.

Social institutions can collapse from within or be captured from without. Their power and wealth are preyed upon from both directions. Institutional values embedded in institutional culture help keep the institution on its focus during leadership changes. It is typical for the founder of an organization to embody its goals based on the social need it was intended to serve. However, when the founder dies, the next person who steps in often views the position as a job, a source of personal revenue. Financial income takes priority over the institutional mission if there is no transmission of institutional values through the institutional structure.

The classical movie theme about the spoiled son that inherits his father's company and spends it into bankruptcy applies to the destruction of any social institution from within. The decline of Rome with Commodus is such a case. Commodus was more concerned with his appeal to the Roman citizen than focusing on their well-being.

The continuity of institutional mission and values is frequently threatened from without. An economic or government takeover of a hospital dedicated to the Hippocratic Oath and focused on saving people's lives will inevitably turn into a hospital that rations care. If it is an economic takeover, priority is given to serving those who can pay more. Also, an effort will be put into selling services the patient does not need. This is because the new owner's primary of mission is making money, not saving lives. If a government takes over a hospital, the managers will try to offer equal service to all citizens at the lowest cost. There will be no competition under a monopoly. Good and bad doctors will get paid the same, and innovation aimed at saving life will disappear. The patient will not be able to make any sovereign decisions about healthcare but accept institutional fate like a serf.

Trubshaw states that "all institutions face three external threats: long-term viability, susceptibility to risk-taking, and ideological capture."[6] Ideological capture is cultural, but economic and governmental capture are both possible. All three forms of capture can destroy an institution unless its culture remains focused on its original mission. The natural tendency of the leader of an institution is to manage those it serves rather than serve sovereign individuals. The temptation of institutional leaders to use an institution to serve other purposes must always be checked.

Personal and Impersonal Institutions

Personal social institutions need to be understood differently from impersonal ones. Personal relations are face-to-face. They can target services to the specific need of individuals. Impersonal relations treat each person as a unit, and justice demands that everyone be treated equally.

This distinction separates family and community from a bureaucratic state or a life insurance company. The personal relationship between a patient and a doctor is very different from that between an actuary in a health insurance company and the patient. The doctor will want to provide the best treatment based on personal knowledge of the patient's health. A health insurance company or government health plan is motivated to pay for the minimum required service and ration treatment. A pharmaceutical company will want to sell its products to as many people as possible whether they need them or not. Those relations are impersonal, and often processed by answers on forms. A doctor in private practice depends on the individual patients, who will return and recommend others if the doctor has a good reputation.

A doctor assigned by an institution will be more motivated to make his employer happy than the patient. However, a small community-level practice is more likely to treat patients as sovereign individuals because their success is based on personal relations in the community.

Face-to-face communities, families, local businesses, and clubs are naturally inclined to treat individuals as sovereigns. These institutions

6. Ibid., p. 28.

remain under the control of sovereign individuals. The same principle applies to community schools and police whose paychecks depend on serving parents of students and local property owners. Schools funded by a state are more likely to indoctrinate, unless the state money is given as vouchers that parents can use to shop for the best instruction.

Social institutions that serve thousands or millions of people anonymously can try to be more friendly through customer service, but they will not make decisions based on individual needs. A large auto manufacturer will not design cars for one individual; a government will not make a law for one person; a national TV network will not broadcast news based on the interests of one listener. These relations are impersonal, each buyer, citizen, or viewer is treated as a number, and decisions are often made by statistical analyses. Impersonal institutions cannot provide personal care, and it is a mistake to expect it.

Aristotle addressed personal and impersonal relations when critiquing Plato's *Republic:*

> Property that is common to the greatest number of owners receives the least attention; men care most for their private possessions, and for what they own in common less, or only so far as it falls to their own individual share for in addition to the other reasons, they think less of it on the ground that someone else is thinking about it, just as in household service a large number of domestics sometimes give worse attendance than a smaller number. And it results in each citizen's having a thousand sons, and these do not belong to them as individuals but any child is equally the son of anyone, so that all alike will regard them with indifference.[7]

City, county, and state governments are impersonal bureaucracies. Justice requires them to be blind and treat everyone equally, regardless of race, creed, or sex. Governments are unable to care for people in a personal way. Care is still impersonal, even if they try to break people down into groups by statistics. A bureaucracy does not know if a person is happy

---

7. Aristotle, *The Politics,* Book II. http://www.perseus.tufts.edu/hopper/text?doc=Perseus:abo:tlg,0086,035:2.

or sad, sick or well, or has a severe need. They only see data on forms. To expect a state to provide personal services with impersonal equipment is to put social consciousness on the wrong level.

LEVELS AND SPHERES OF SOCIETY

Society consists of many levels. Personal levels are family and community. Larger institutions, cities, states, and federal and world-level institutions are impersonal. Keeping social institutions at the appropriate level is vital for their function.

In an integral society, there is an appropriate measure of sovereignty related to each level. Like the sovereignty of the individual should be served by any social institutions, the lower level social institutions should be served by the higher. This principle has been well-articulated in Catholic Church teaching on the principle of subsidiarity:

> A community of a higher order should not interfere in the internal life of a community of a lower order, depriving the latter of its functions, but rather should support it in case of need and help to co- ordinate its activity with the activities of the rest of society, always with a view to the common good.[8]

A pyramid represents a stable structure, where upper levels rest on the lower, with each level being smaller than the one below it. The Egyptian pyramids remain after thousands of years because of their stable pyramid structure. A stable society is bottom-up, built on large numbers of sovereign individuals contributing to the production that makes social institutions possible.

Subsidiarity is not the best term to describe the relationship of levels from an integral perspective. In the corporate world, a subsidiary company is spun off from the top, indicating a top-down flow of authority. While pushing for the greatest responsibility at the lowest possible level,

---

8. Pius XI, Quadragesimo anno I, (1883)184-186. In Catholic doctrine, all social bodies exist for the individual, who is sovereign. Responsibility should fall on the lowest level of society possible.

the Catholic Church, has a long tradition of top-down dictates and rejection of feedback from below. The response to Martin Luther's criticism of indulgences and the Copernican theory that the earth revolves around the sun are examples of institutional resistance to change.

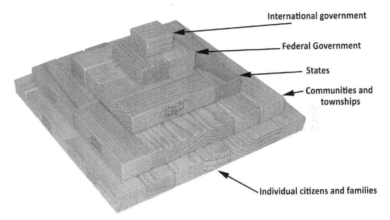

Figure 2: A stable social order is built on sovereign individuals and each higher level is smaller and depends on the lower.

A state is a *voluntary* union, while a "province" is a subdivision from above. And a "federation" should be a voluntary union of institutions, with each having the right to secede if the costs of membership outweigh the benefits.

When the sovereignty of a state is considered more important than its individuals, and the social system is organized from the top-down through force, the state is inherently unstable. First, it is unable to personally nurture individuals to best function at the lowest level. An impersonal attempt to nurture always creates structural oppression. Secondly, a top-heavy social system puts more pressure on lower levels creating instability. If the system is centralized and fails, everyone dependent on it will suffer.

Compare the vulnerability of individuals and families that produce their energy to the vulnerability of those who rely on energy from a grid managed by a public utility. If energy production is decentralized one person's power goes out, nobody else will suffer. However, if the central grid goes down in the winter, nobody will have power and many people are likely to freeze to death. Further, a state is more vulnerable to external attack if the enemy knocks out a centralized grid. Again, all the citizens are vulnerable. However, if energy production is decentralized, an attack on one point on the grid will not cause widespread harm.

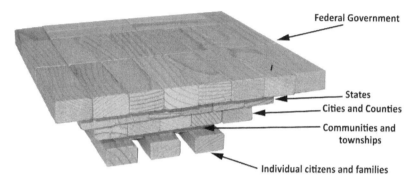

Figure 3: In a sovereign state system, the highest government feeds off lower levels, causing structural oppression.

Compare the economic security of a state with one bank, or a few big banks, to a state with three thousand small banks. If a central bank fails, the entire population might lose their money. If one of three thousand banks fail, most people won't notice.

Almost any human need—energy, money, police, education—is best served, and social institutions most resilient, when decentralization is maximized to the lowest possible social level. A society that champions individual sovereignty will promote as much decentralization and personal responsibility as possible.

Irresponsible or non-productive individuals and social institutions desire to push for centralization on the mistaken assumption that it is easier for a higher level to manage problems because they may have more power or money. Politicians love to pander to non-productive individuals on promises of taking care of their needs to get votes. Cultures, or news media, that foster such thinking lead to social failure.

Lower levels should not pass off responsibilities to higher levels, For example, a city should not expect a state to manage residential water bills. However, states should be involved in regulating water use in rivers that flow through several cities. Homeowners should not expect the city government to plow their driveway. Conversely, upper levels should not usurp responsibilities that lower levels can do.

Levels exist in all social spheres: culture, economy, and governance. In an integral society, there is not only an appropriate level for a social institution but an appropriate sphere. When studying social institutions from an integral perspective, it is essential to (1) know which sphere they belong to, (2) know the lowest level where they can function, and (3) know the limitations that enable an institution to serve its purpose without causing harm to others.

THE INTEGRAL STATE

The Treaty of Westphalia (1648), signed by Holy Roman emperor Ferdinand III, other German princes, France, and Sweden, initiated the modern state system.[9] Peace was negotiated after the 80 years Spanish-Dutch war and 30 years of war in Germany. This treaty guaranteed the territorial sovereignty of states, the central authority of the emperor, who ceded sovereignty to about 300 princes and upheld the freedom of conscience. It required religious toleration of Lutherans, Calvinists, and Catholics and guaranteed emigration for people of other religions. In addition to giving territorial sovereignty to a lower level of governance, it provided more cultural autonomy for individuals seeking truth through reading and reflection. England, Poland, Russia, and the Ottoman Empire kept traditional state religions and did not sign the Treaty.[10]

In 1579, seven territories in the modern Netherlands broke away from Spain, forming an alliance for common defense at the treaty of Utrecht. They created the Republic of the Seven United Netherlands,

---

9. "Peace of Westphalia," *Encyclopedia Brittanica*. https://www.britannica.com/event/Peace-of-Westphalia.

10. Ibid.

known as the Dutch Republic, in 1588. Small independent states that championed the freedom of thought and religious tolerance voluntarily federated, and power flowed from the bottom-up. Artists, science, and trade flourished under these freedoms, and the 17th century became the Dutch Golden Age.

The Dutch provinces were further politically decentralized in towns, providing checks against the centralization of political power. Regents from the merchant elite ran these towns, claiming to act for the citizenry.[11] There was not broad political participation, but the regents were accountable to citizens through face-to-face relations.

The U.S. Confederation of States began similarly as a league of colonies organized to overthrow British rule. In the U.S., the town or township, like a British Parish, had significant territorial sovereignty, taking responsibility for public utilities and roads. Towns and counties were the primary focus of the government of most American citizens, and there was a high degree of democratic participation. The states had little resources to pay off war debts, and the Confederation had little power to organize a country.

James Madison represented the sentiment of many Americans when he criticized the Dutch system for its lack of citizen participation in *The Federalist* numbers 10 and 20.[12] The U.S. Founders sought to create a more centralized system that included a union of states and a check on the power of elites by the citizens. Their hybrid system of government had citizen representation at the federal level. This was like the direct participation of the plebs in 35 districts in the ancient Roman Republic but checked by my skilled officials in the Senate. The states could not create a union of elites because they were checked by sovereign citizens. States appointed representatives to the Senate, which had more direct

---

11. Joerg Knipprath, "United Provinces of the Netherlands and the Articles of Confederation: Factors Influencing Design Toward a Stable U.S. Constitution," Constituting America. https://constitutingamerica.org/90day-aer-united-provinces-netherlands-and-articles-of-confederation-factors-influencing-design-toward-a-stable-us-constitution-guest-essayist-joerg-knipprath/

12. Ibid.

influence over the federal administration, but the people could control their spending through the lower house. The upper and lower houses have veto power over each other's legislation.

The Dutch and U.S. Republics both prospered because of the practical recognition of individual sovereignty, whether there was a formal representation of citizens or not. In the West, after France's direct democracy and mob rule failed, the formal recognition of both the right to vote and checks and balances on mob rule became essential principles for the governance of liberal democracies.

In *Perpetual Peace* (1795), Immanuel Kant's first definitive article for perpetual peace is that "the civil constitution of every state should be Republican." Republicanism meant (1) freedom of all citizens, (2) agreement to common legislation, and (3) equality under the law.[13] He argued that governments were either republican or despotic. Simple democracies are despotic because they represented the will of the majority and do not protect the rights of minorities.

The evolution of the modern state has not advanced beyond these republican principles, which are necessary but insufficient for an integral state. An integral state requires the government referee society's cultural and economic spheres. Western liberal democracies protect cultural sovereignty through freedoms of thought and speech and political sovereignty through the right to vote. Still, they have not developed constitutions with checks and balances on economic power that enable the economic sovereignty of citizens. The constitutions of integral states need to include articles related to financial conflicts of interest in governance, money, and banking.

This chapter started with concerns about the devastating effects of the unchecked power of any social institution—governance, cultural, and economic. The evolution of modern history has provided better mechanisms for preventing the abuses of political and cultural power than in the economy. One such check, the Glass-Steagall Act, was highlighted

---

13. Immanuel Kant, *Perpetual Peace,* ed. Lewis White Beck (Indianapolis: IN: Boobs-Merrill, 1975), p. 11..

in the section on institutional viruses and hijacking. However, the Act's value, and the importance of other checks in the economic sphere, have not become embedded in modern social consciousness. Facilitating individual economic sovereignty through necessary reform is more fully discussed in Chapters 11 and 12.

An International Federation of Free States

The next level above the state is the Federation of States. The United States, the European Union, the Russian Federation, and several regional alliances represent this level of governance. Some of these Federations stem from voluntary participation, others by force. Immanuel Kant's second definitive article for perpetual peace is that "the law of nations shall be founded on a federation of free states."[14]

Kant's view of voluntary membership of states implies the right to secede. In a society of voluntary participation from the bottom up, each level has greater sovereignty than the level above it. Citizens have more sovereignty than states. States have more sovereignty than their Federations, and federations have more sovereignty than global institutions.

In an integral world society, rulers would be restrained by laws that forbade aggression and higher levels of governance checked by the right of secession.[15] Such a bottom-up approach to international governance is necessary for peace.

> ...there must be a league of a particular kind, which can be called a league of peace *(foedus pacificum)*... This league does not tend to any dominion over the power of the state but only to the maintenance and security of the freedom of the state itself.[16]

In a social organization, members cede limited and temporary sovereignty to the organization in exchange for membership benefits. A

---

14. Ibid, p. 16.

15. Gordon L. Anderson, "The Right to Secede," *Life, Liberty, and the Pursuit of Happiness, Version 4.0,* (St. Paul, MN: Paragon House, 2009), pp. 149-173.

16. Immanuel Kant, *Perpetual Peace*, p. 18.

league of states could offer a state greater security at a lower cost than securing all its borders at its own expense. But if the League should become oppressive, a state should be able to withdraw. Kant considered this voluntary bottom-up association to be pushed by a "cunning of history" because, even though survival instincts are to conquer, social-ization leads to cooperation. States, like children in a sandbox, will be pushed by the cunning of history to learn to play together for mutual happiness. This socialization process from barbaric to civilized behavior develops at all levels of society. Finally, socialization at the global level will lead to an integral commons after attempts by bully powers to dom-inate the world learn to live together.

The Hague conferences were the first attempt to hold states account-able worldwide. In 1899, Tsar Nicholas II of Russia opened the first Hague Conference. The conference adopted several international con-ventions. The most prominent was the establishment of a Permanent Court of Arbitration, ratified by 26 states: all major world powers and several smaller states. Participation in the Court was *voluntary* to avoid violating state sovereignty. Disputing states had to both agree to accept the verdict of the Court before submitting to arbitration. Conventions were adopted regarding the rules of war and arms, but the US, UK, and China did not ratify them all.

A second conference was held in 1907 at the urging of U.S. President Theodore Roosevelt. He won the Nobel Prize in 1905 for negotiating the Treaty of Portsmouth between the Russians and the Chinese. The Treaty considered the two major powers, but not the rights of the peo-ple they ruled. The independence-seeking Koreans were "given" to the Japanese, violating the principle of subsidiarity and ignoring individual sovereignty, leading to frustration and violence.

The 1907 Conference expanded the 1899 conventions that the United Nations later adopted. The Geneva Conventions added to this body of international law, now ratified by over 100 states. In the first decade of the 20th century, the liberal world was optimistic toward world peace through arbitration. Hope was dashed by real abuses of unchecked state power. Member states were unable to hold rogue states in check.

WWI broke out in 1914 as bully states ignored the process of arbitration. After the First World War, the League of Nations was founded by members who agreed to abstain from war. But some states did not live up to their word. Italy and Germany violated the conventions without consequence. The Kellogg-Briand Pact was negotiated in 1928, but it was also soon broken.

World War II convinced the world that rogue states had to be checked by military power. The United Nations upgraded the League of Nations, adding an International Security Council of great powers that could act as peacekeepers. Five great powers agreed to protect smaller states if rogue states invaded. However, the great powers on the Security Council (1) failed to remain neutral and (2) failed to obey just war conventions. They all had veto power on the Council, but were exempt from actions taken by the other four. The five great powers remained unchecked.

The United Nations' created global governance institutions, but these bodies did not remain referees. They became players in the international economy and culture. A result was the rise of an international order that rewarded dictators and tyrants who received money from the International Monetary Fund (IMF) or other forms of assistance. The member governments argued that technical and financial assistance from the UN for less-developed states had to be given to state governments, not directly to economic producers.[17] This aid increased the power of those state governments, reducing their need to rely on or serve the citizens. Many republican states turned into dictatorships. Money intended for development in the 1960s and 1970s often ended up in the Swiss bank accounts of the UN-created dictators.

Peace researcher Johann Galtung called these leaders dependent on international political/economic hegemony "the center within the periphery."[18] In the name of doing good through honoring state sovereignty, United Nations' economic policies caused instability, oppression,

17. Richard M. Fagley, "The United Nations and Technical Assistance," National Council of Churches Department of International Justice and Goodwill, 1949, p. 3.
18. John Galtung, "A Structural Theory of Imperialism," *Journal of Peace Research*, Vol. 8, No. 2 (Sage Publication, 1971), pp. 81-117.

and even civil wars within states. When UN Peacekeeping missions were not very successful in policing within-state problems, citizens within the states viewed it as an occupation that ignored their sovereignty.

Without neutral and conscientious great powers, the principle of state sovereignty proved unenforceable and detrimental to world peace. The United Nations, despite its intentions, undermined the stability of its member states by ignoring the sovereignty of individuals.

INDIVIDUAL SOVEREIGNTY AS THE STARTING POINT OF PEACE

People are not happy as servants of their governments or a world order that prevents the natural pursuit of life, family, property, and happiness. People resist slavery to other people and social institutions. They will voluntarily join and serve social institutions that enable their pursuit of life, liberty, and property. School boards, stock investments, churches, scout troops, 4-H clubs, fraternities, and other organizations attract such voluntary membership. If such organizations are hijacked or fail, people will naturally leave them and stop funding them.

Whenever power is imposed from above by a state without the voluntary consent of the citizens, structural oppression, suffering, and even genocide follow. The ability of individuals to pursue happiness depends on whether social institutions enable that pursuit or exploit those they should serve. In leadership, this is the distinction made between a "statesman" and a "politician."

CONCLUSION

Social institutions should be considered sovereign only for limited social purposes. A state is sovereign in providing security for its territory and acting as a referee in other areas. In acting as referees, governance institutions should consider individuals, not institutions, as sovereigns. Integral social institutions are created through a voluntary, bottom-up approach, not by conquest and imposition by a higher will. A resilient society depends on keeping social institutions focused on their mission and preventing the expansion, hijacking, or infection that subverts their mission.

The U.S. Declaration of Independence and the Constitution were created by and for sovereign individuals and aided the cause of ending slavery and disenfranchisement of women. A Constitution guaranteeing rights is not sufficient for the individual pursuit of happiness. Individual sovereignty includes self-direction, self-reliance, and self-governance. Social institutions assist people when they support sovereign individuals, remain true to their mission, and in the proper place in society.

When the U.S. Declaration of Independence was issued, society mainly consisted of sovereign individuals and families. Townships were the backbone of American governance.[19] Big corporations like the Hudson's Bay Company and the East India Company had been outlawed. This was a world of individuals more sovereign than today. It was an integral society in an earlier stage of social evolution.

That world of individual sovereignty has been displaced by complex social institutions originally intended to serve that sovereignty. But such institutions are routinely hijacked by institutional viruses that exploit individuals. Defense against such viruses and keeping social institutions focused on their mission are primary challenges of our time.

Chapter 9 looks at some of these challenges in the governance sphere, focusing on the division of legislative power. Chapter 10 will look at the place of cultural institutions, and Chapters 11 and 12 look at economic institutions.

---

19. Alexis DeToqueville, *Democracy in America,* op. cit.

Chapter 9

Elites and the People: Legislation in an Integral Society

ELITES: QUALIFIED AND ACCOUNTABLE

Social institutions are organized to serve specific purposes. They need people qualified to lead them. And these leaders need to be held accountable, particularly leaders in government. How can this be done?

The structure of a social institution flows from its purpose, but there will always be elites and people. The elite could be the owners of a business and the people the employees. The elite could be a school board and administrators, and the people teachers and students. The elite could be the leaders of a government agency and the people, the staff, and citizens the agency serves.

The elite must have the knowledge and skills in all these different institutions to carry out the institutional mission. Too often, they do not. Inheritance is not proof of qualification. Commodus did not have the skills to be the Emperor of Rome. Loyalty is not proof of qualification. An appointee in charge of an agency for loyalty rather than skill, is likely to sidetrack the agency's activity and cause it to waste funds or fail its mission. Promises are not proof of qualification. A political candidate may promise everything to voters, but often they don't have the skills or resources to deliver on those promises.

Passing a test showing knowledge of the history and rules of the institution can help. Having good grades in a school providing training in the field can help. Having previous success leading a comparable institution is better than training. Experience should be top on the list of the people who choose leaders.

Once leaders are in place, how are the kept accountable for their performance in their mission? "Who guards the guardians?"[1] Accountability should be based on job performance metrics. Is the institution improving on delivering its product? Accounting, record keeping, and transparency are required. Leaders who hide data, operate in secret, and blame others when goals are not met are usually not performing their job successfully or misusing institutional resources.

While there are natural disasters and occasional reasons to classify documents, secrecy is generally a sign of leadership failure. Investigative journalists consider this behavior a primary reason to investigate an institution, particularly a government official or agency.

INSTITUTIONAL FEEDBACK

Resilient social institutions follow metrics related to their mission. Metrics are the primary indicator of institutional success. The performance of the entire institution, not just the leaders, is judged by metrics. Metrics can be applied to leaders, the people who work for the institution and the people served by it—customers, citizens, and others.

Responsible workers provide feedback to leaders when they see possible improvements. Responsible leaders need to listen to that feedback. The 9/11 attacks may have been prevented if FBI leadership had better listened to field agents in Minneapolis. They wanted to investigate the laptop of Zacarias Moussaoui, who had been arrested with evidence he was involved with plots to hijack airplanes. In a 13-page letter to her boss, FBI Director Robert Mueller, Christine Rowley, the FBI Minneapolis legal division counsel, wrote:

---

1. *Quis custodiet ipsos custodes?* is the phrase used by Juvenal in *Satires* (Satire VI, lines 347–348) in first century Rome. Discussion of the topic can be found in Plato's *Republic*.

Hopefully, with our nation's security on the line, you and our nation's other elected and appointed officials can rise above the petty politics that often plague other discussions and do the right thing. You do have some good ideas for change in the FBI but I think you have also not been completely honest about some of the true reasons for the FBI's pre-September 11th failures. Until we come clean and deal with the root causes, the Department of Justice will continue to experience problems fighting terrorism and fighting crime in general.[2]

Rowley made the *Time Magazine* cover with two other whistle-blowers that year, but Mueller, a political appointee, classified and buried the memo. Whistle-blowers are a symptom of institutional leadership failure and inadequate institutional feedback mechanisms. When people expose wrong-doing in a government, they can suffer severely. Edward Snowden and Julian Assange are high-profile individuals who leaked classified documents that exposed illegal behavior by intelligence agencies. Institutional feedback and greater transparency are necessary to keep such agencies honest and focused on their mission. A higher bar for document classification and greater punishment when people classify documents to protect themselves should be required.

Problems of transparency are everywhere because people naturally try hide their mistakes from others as a form of self-defense. Workers hide mistakes from bosses, and bosses hide mistakes from their employers. Thr failure to report a defective o-ring on the Space Shuttle launch rocket or of a manager to listen to the report can have catastrophic consequences for the National Space Agency. Such feedback failures have life-and-death consequences.

Sustainable societies must be intelligently led and serve the needs of all people, "the masses." Only a tiny percentage of the population makes up the ruling class. But, without proper checks and balances, political elites, the guardians, will inevitably use their power to become lords and masters and treat the masses as slaves, serfs, and expendables. On the other hand,

---

2. Lauren Robinson, "Protectiong the Rights of Whistle-Blowers," *Social Education* 69(6), pg 313–317 ©2005 National Council for the Social Studies.

democracies inevitably fail because the masses try to use the government as a provider rather than limiting the government to the role of referee.

Legislation is crucial for the good governance of a society. The laws should not represent all desires of the people or the leaders, but bounded by principles that protect individual sovereignty and referee civil disputes. Feedback is required between those who administer the law, those who make the law, and the people the law serves. This is necessary for a resilient government.

THE EVOLUTION OF LEGISLATIVE INSTITUTIONS

The division of government power into three branches has been an essential step in the evolution of society. In early civilizations, the King was the rule-maker, administrator, and judge. These functions can be united with good results in face-to-face families and tribes but are inappropriate for larger societies that must govern citizens impersonally and impartially.

Each branch of government is an institution with a specific purpose. The legislature makes the laws, the administration executes the laws, and the judiciary settles disputes by applying the law. Each institution has elites who should have qualifications, and there should be a way to hold them accountable. Each branch of government needs good feedback mechanisms that serve sovereign citizens in their pursuit of happiness.

The courts in British and American law rely on precedent. A precedent is a mechanism of feedback that enables evolution in the adjudication of the law. Administrative agencies that enforce the law need their power limited by the legislative and judicial branches. Neither the administrative branch nor the judiciary should make laws. The legislature can call executive rules and judicial decisions out of bounds by making laws that override them.

In Ancient Rome, the legislative and administrative branches of government were separated. The Senate served as the legislative body representing a confederation of tribal landholders. The Consul served as head of the administration and was primarily charged with the security of the Republic.

The division of power provided freedom for the people to prosper. As the population grew, the society formed into two social classes, the *patricians,* who descended from the original landholders, and the *plebs* (people), who were an immigrant working class and descendants of freed slaves. Laws passed by the Senate did not represent the plebs, who had no voice in the government. The Senate passed legislation that burdened the masses or provided the elite with special privileges. This bias is a typical problem of elites and masses in any social institution that does not have checks and balances on the elites and feedback from the masses.

A significant historical legislative development occurred after the plebs went on a nationwide strike and forced patricians to allow representatives of the plebs to approve or veto the laws. Both classes approved the *Twelve Tables,* and the Council of Plebs and its Tribunes brought checks, balances, and feedback to the legislative branch of government.

A similar development occurred in England, although in England the King originally had absolute power. In the 11th century, the kings consulted witans (councils) made up of ecclesiastical leaders and government ministers. Then the king was pressed to sign the *Magna Carta* (1215) that paralleled the Twelve Tables of Rome in guaranteeing rights, protections, and due process for all free men. The councils became the House of Lords,[3] and the House of Commons became a second house that could present grievances from people who were not nobles.

Over time, with the rise in wealth and influence of the commercial class, the House of Commons became the primary legislative body and controlled taxation, similar to the House of Representatives in the United States. However, the House of Commons should not function like a unicameral legislature. There should be checks on the will of the masses from hijacking the government, e.g., the form of government should be republican, not simple democracy.

The legislative system in Germany better maintains distinct bodies representing different interests of elites and masses. The *Bundestag*

---

3. "House of Lords," *Encyclopedia Britannica.* https://www.britannica.com/topic/House-of-Lords

consists of elected representatives of the people, while the *Bundesrat* represents the sixteen Länder (federated states) of Germany at the federal level. The main problem with the German system is that the administrative branch can also introduce legislation. Even though either the Bundestag or the Bundesrat can effectively veto a bill, the German system will tend to become an administrative state that undermines individual sovereignty. Further, German political parties receive government funding and serve as a channel for special interest legislation, undermining individual sovereignty.

The U.S. Founders could quickly agree that the lower house would consist of representatives of the people. However, they were divided over who would make up the Senate and how Senators are elected. These discussions almost derailed the Convention. The "Great Compromise" concluded with two Senators appointed by each state.[4] Each state had equal representation, but smaller states received greater proportional representation, frustrating larger states.

The Senate would represent people experienced in governance in the states. Senators would be able to serve as a check against "mob rule" by representatives of the masses in the House of Representatives. Senators could also serve as a check on moneyed interests and panderers that could mislead voters and bankrupt the government. However, special interests were not adequately contained over the long run.

The 17th Amendment to the Constitution destroyed the Founder's system of checks and balances in the legislative process. The Amendment replaced the state appointment of Senators with the election of Senators by citizens. Essentially, both houses became houses of the plebs. This made the Senate a superfluous political body and eliminated elites with professional skills from the legislative process. Further, states no longer had direct representation in their own Federation. The same result would have come from eliminating the Senate and having a unicameral legislature.

---

4. Catherine Drinker Bowen, *Miracle at Philadelphia: The Story of the Constitutional Convention May to September 1787* (Boston: Little, Brown, 1966, 1986) pp. 185-187,

The 17th Amendment removed a check on the harm that the people could do to their own government. It changed the form of government from a Republic to a more simple type of democracy that has consistently failed. Popular legislation is not checked by qualified experts.

Further, political parties, special interests, and government administrators have hijacked the legislative process. Omnibus legislation has enabled bills to be stuffed with special interest legislation that does not represent the consent of the governed.

Finally, political parties essentially "own" the peoples' representatives after they are elected because party affiliation is listed on ballots. When given such ballots, people generally vote for a party slate, rather than a representative. This ensures that candidates on the ballot will be loyal to political parties. If candidates do not vote on legislation in lockstep with their party, they will not receive an endorsement in the next election. Removing party names from ballots would be a straightforward method of returning the loyalty of representatives to their constituents rather than party donor interests. Party names on ballots contribute to partisan tribalism.

Inadequately structured legislative processes exist in most countries. Most countries list party names on ballots. In most countries, the government is a player, not a referee. Legislation is not in the interest of individual sovereignty but financial interests, ideological interests, and politicians with large egos who would hijack government and economic resources for personal and group ends.

SENATE REPRESENTATION OF THE THREE CULTURAL SPHERES

Since before the ancient empire of Babylon, kings and emperors had spiritual, economic, and governance advisors. Wisdom from all three social spheres went into the decisions for making laws. The House of Lords in England, the upper house, represented two social spheres, the cultural sphere through ecclesiastical advisors and the governance sphere through ministers. The House of Commons represented knights and burgesses, members of the military, and the townspeople.[5] The burgesses represented the interests of the merchant class. But, merchants needed military protection and happy consumers, so they also represented their interests.

In the Roman Republic, the Senate was composed of representatives of the patricians, whose interests were checked by the tribunes that represented the interests of the plebs. Then, after the Conflict of Orders, the People's Assembly was divided into 35 districts based on territory. Representatives of these territories represented both the rich and the poor. In the late Republic, these assemblies had more lawmaking influence than the Senate. The Republic eventually fell into civil wars as politicians pandered to the people with promises that ruined the economy and governance system. There was never any specific representation of social spheres in the legislative process.

The United States, and later the German Republic, had an upper house composed of government representatives appointed by states or Länder. They had expertise in governance but not the cultural or economic sphere. Such a system works well in a society where individuals have cultural and economic sovereignty but not in a society where large social and financial institutions like investment funds, banks, social media, and tech giants have stripped that sovereignty away.

One way to fix this imbalance is for representatives of each cultural sphere in a Senate. Each state would have three senators. One would represent the cultural sphere—philosophers, religious leaders, and social scientists. A second would be a representative of the economic sphere—business and industry leaders. A third would represent state governance. The state legislature could appoint the governance Senator, however economic and cultural leaders would better be chosen by state-level economic and cultural institutions. Cultural and financial experts on a Senate would help ensure government stayed a referee in those spheres.

---

5. "House of Commons," *Encyclopedia Britannica.* https://www.britannica.com/topic/House-of-Commons-British-government

LEGISLATIVE BODIES TO REPRESENT BOTH ELITES AND MASSES

This brief review of the history of legislation in the West leads to the conclusion that legislation should consider all the elements of an integral society. The sovereignty of individual citizens is represented by a lower house and social institutions represented by the upper house. These two houses, with the power to veto one another, provide checks and balances so the lower house can prevent the abuse of individual sovereignty while the upper house can prevent the destruction or misuse of social institutions.

Each house needs to be kept on its institutional mission. Laws are required to prevent political parties or other groups from hijacking the political power of the masses in the lower house. Senatorial candidates should be professionals in all three social spheres and chosen by a process that selects based on expertise, not on election by the masses.

This structural division of one body representing people's rights and the other representing institutional responsibilities. This division will allow the Senate to veto dysfunctional popular demands, while the house can veto legislation that would oppress individual citizens. Today Western culture emphasizes rights, but societies require both rights and responsibilities. Liberal democracies can improve their legislative institutions when both rights and responsibilities are structured into the legislative process.

Asian culture has emphasized responsibilities over rights. Obligations are embedded into the Confucian cultural traditions. Chinese leaders have abused these traditions by demanding loyalty and ignoring human rights. The Chinese Communist Party functions like a Senate, representing political elites. Adding a house of representatives representing the people, would bring a check against human rights abuses.

The Chinese system of civil exams initiated in the sixth century, aided the stability of the empire for a thousand years and provided a vehicle for social mobility.[6] Civil service exams related to the three cultural spheres would improve on this process, but practical experience, e.g. academic professorship, business success, and previous government leadership, would also be important for the best functioning Senate.

CONCLUSION

In an integral society, the making of law is just one branch of governance. The judicial and administrative branches involve "refereeing" the law. Policing and regulating the cultural and economic spheres is the critical role of government that enables citizens to pursue happiness.

This chapter has focused on structural reforms to make lawmaking and social governance more integral. Structural reforms occur in social institutions that manifest the social consciousness, which is the interior dimension of a social institution. On Ken Wilber's four quadrants diagram (Figure 5, Appendix), this means the lower two quadrants should be put to the service of the upper two quadrants, enabling the development of sovereign individuals.

---

6. "The Confucian Classics & the Civil Service Examinations," Weatherhead East Asian Institute, Columbia University. http://afe.easia.columbia.edu/cosmos/irc/classics.htm

Chapter

10

Ethical Institutional Culture

The morals of property and the family were spread, and came to dominate a large part of the world, not because those who accepted them were able rationally to convince others that they were correct, and certainly not because they themselves liked them, but because those groups who by accident did accept them prospered and multiplied more than others.[1]

Cultural evolution is not necessarily rational. Much of the "truth" that guides human society reflects pragmatic social success—what works. Reason and science have evolved as a reflection on the world and human interaction with it. Social institutions like the family and private property are spontaneous institutions arising from the nature of human life and the social interactions of sovereign individuals.

The family is the organic social institution that has arisen in response to the natural instinct for sex, reproduction, and raising children resulting from sexual union. Families exist in tribes that precede civilizations. Ownership of property is a natural result of the instinct for stable housing and the desire to exchange goods and services. Without institutional rules related to family and property, individuals cannot channel these instincts into socially peaceful, constructive, and productive behavior. Such laws enable individual sovereignty in large impersonal societies.

---

1. Frederick A. Hayek, "The Presumption of Reason," draft prepared for the 14th International Conference on the Unity of the Sciences, Houston, Texas, 1985. © 1986, International Cultural Foundation,

The traditional transmission of social rules related to family and property in society has been justified as the word of God or the will of heaven. Modern scientism tries to discredit such rules because the religious justification seems arbitrary or relative to the rational mind. However, that misses the point that some traditional principles are universal, transcendent, and a product of cultural evolution. Religion was how these principles were conveyed. The primary point is that these rules transcend the arbitrary laws of individual leaders of social institutions. Like gravity is a law of nature, "thou shall not kill or steal" are laws of civilized society. Such laws apply to all people everywhere.

The ancient Mesopotamian and Biblical codes were not the arbitrary proclamations of rulers or religions. They cannot be discarded because someone did not prove them with reason. Still, rational intellectuals want more proof for the laws we develop today, especially since the rules are not exactly the same in different cultures we have inherited. This has also led to moral and ethical relativism.

The ancient Greeks and Romans also wrestled with the problem of choosing "whose rules and why?" Ethical and moral relativism is a problem whenever there is a confluence of cultures, such as in a cosmopolitan city or large empire. Hayek began to address this issue with his pragmatic observation that societies that valued the family and private property "prospered and multiplied more than others." This observation can be corroborated with social science studies based on metrics.

MORALITY AND ETHICS

While morality and ethics are often used interchangeably, there are some subtle differences in the terms. Morality is a word that has been used by the Church and religious leaders in instruction related to personal behavior, particularly in one's actions towards others in ways that could cause personal harm to life or property: murder, theft, and family responsibilities.

Ethics is a term more often used in business and government and usually refers to behavior that could impact a social institution. Conflicts of interest in which a person can use a position in an institution to personally gain, usually at the expense of others, are one of the most common ethical issues. They generally fall into the category of theft, not the direct theft of another's personal property, but an indirect theft to unethical use of institutional resources.

Ethical issues related to murder and sex also arise in social institutions. A hostile takeover of a company that intends to destroy it and gain a monopoly could be considered institutional murder. Hostile takeovers do not directly murder individuals, but they can destroy the lives of those being put out of work. Using one's institutional position as a boss to extract sexual or other favors from employees is unethical. This is extortion in an institutional setting.

In conclusion, it is necessary to discuss both personal and institutional wrongdoing. The terms moral and ethical behavior help make this distinction. Immorality would be disobedience of standards of personal goodness, while unethical behavior is using an institutional position in a way that causes harm to others or the social institution.

CULTURAL EVOLUTION

In his book *Developmental Politics,*[2] Steve McIntosh discusses philosophical evolution in the cultural sphere. He describes how to transcend the cultural polarization in the contemporary world through the integration of traditional values and virtues, modernism, and post-modernism. The machinery of current political systems is driven by interests fighting over the resources of government and not values.

> Values are easier to integrate than interests because an authentic bedrock value is something that almost everyone already shares.[3]

In addition to revisiting the values of truth, beauty, and goodness, McIntosh develops a co-evolved value of virtue. "Values are the best of

---

2. Steve McIntosh, *Developmental Politics: How America Can Grow Into a Better Version of Itself* (St. Paul, MN: Paragon House, 2020).

3. Ibid., p. 61.

what we want, but virtues are the best of who we are."[4] The search for value and practice of improving virtue stimulates transcendence. "The practice of virtue can become a politically unifying force in American culture."[5] Virtuous leadership served the Roman Empire under the five good emperors and can unify Western civilization today. The practice of virtue marks the core difference between a politician and a statesman.

We will not go into the details of McIntosh's excellent analysis of cultural evolution here, but accept its conclusions as an important guide to evolution of the cultural sphere. Leadership rooted in values and virtues us essential for the relationship between individual sovereignty and social institutions as the world evolves towards an integral commons.

ETHICAL LEADERSHIP

Ethical leadership of an institution is as important as one's technical skills and knowledge. Both skill and virtue are necessary attributes of a good leader.

The five good emperors in Rome strove to embody the virtues of stoicism. In his *Meditations,* Marcus Aurelius provides many thoughts about the good and virtuous life: striving for an understanding of the whole and seeing how everything relates; seeking justice and no harm for everyone; using reason and dispassion to avoid a biased or corrupt conclusion; believe a solution is possible, even if you don't immediately see one; and understand what is under your control and what is not:

> Herein doth consist happiness of life, for a man to know thoroughly the true nature of everything; what is the matter, and what is the form of it: with all his heart and soul, ever to do that which is just, and to speak the truth. What then remaineth but to enjoy thy life in a course and coherence of good actions, one upon another immediately succeeding, and never interrupted, though for never so little a while?[6]

---

4. Ibid. p. 130.
5. Ibid. p. 145.
6. Marcus Aurelius, *Meditations,* Book 12:22. https://www.gutenberg.org/files/2680/2680-h/2680-h.htm#link2H_4_0001

The British aristocracy established elite schools like Oxford and Cambridge to teach skill and virtue. Both were considered essential for managing an estate and performing social responsibilities. Prior success in managing an estate was often a requirement for a government post. Greek and Roman leaders were similarly trained. Alexander the Great learned many military skills from his father and general knowledge from Aristotle.

Leaders in modern liberal democratic societies have found stoicism helpful for leadership:

> Many of history's great minds not only understood Stoicism for what it truly is, they sought it out: George Washington, Walt Whitman, Frederick the Great, Eugène Delacroix, Adam Smith, Immanuel Kant, Thomas Jefferson, Matthew Arnold, Ambrose Bierce, Theodore Roosevelt, William Alexander Percy, Ralph Waldo Emerson. Each read, studied, quoted, or admired the Stoics... Marcus Aurelius, Epictetus, Seneca...[7]

Political rhetoricians can be popular and move the masses, but without moral substance and care in executing their responsibilities, they do not provide good leadership after being elected. Responsible citizens in a Republic must look for virtuous character when choosing leaders. The Jewish and Christian traditions promoted many of the ancient virtues that the U.S. founders believed necessary to maintain the Republic:

> We have no government capable of contending with human passions unbridled by morality and religion. Avarice, ambition, revenge, or gallantry would break the strongest cords of our constitution as a whale goes through a net. Our constitution was made only for a moral and religious people. It is wholly inadequate to the government of any other.[8]

Ethical leadership and governance knowledge are the cultural spheres'

7. "What Is Stoicism? A Definition & 9 Stoic Exercises To Get You Started," *The Daily Stoic,* https://dailystoic.com/what-is-stoicism-a-definition-3-stoic-exercises-to-get-you-started/.

8. President John Adams, "Letter to Officers of the First Brigade of the First Militia of Massachussetts, October 11, 1798.

contributions to a government serving sovereign citizens. Ethical leadership should not be confused with obedience to religion. Obedience to others is not leadership, obedience to an integral consciousness is a sign of leadership. The diversity that comes from freedom strengthens society. Before its collapse, Rome was culturally pluralistic, with many different religions and beliefs about God. People worshiped in different ways, and good Emperors strove for a stoic consciousness to lead well.

Stoicism was a pragmatic philosophy about achieving truth, beauty, goodness, and success in the world. It is like Yoga, the perfection of mental clarity and physical health in the individual. Yoga is about the unity of the upper left and right quadrants in Wilber's framework (Figure 1). Perfecting the unity of social consciousness and social institutions (lower left and right quadrants) can be called social yoga.

INSTITUTIONAL AND CONSCIOUSNESS AND BEHAVIOR

Like individual humans, each social institution has an inner nature and an external form. The inner nature involves its purpose, organizing principles, and institutional consciousness. Institutions are social constructions. They are analogous to physical things we build, like houses and automobiles. The end product and its purpose is envisioned, and plans are drawn. The plans for a bridge require knowledge of the strength and durability of materials and assembly methods. The designer must have a an understanding of these principles. Knowledge of social principles is necessary for creating resilient social institutions.

In the physical sciences, different principles apply to various fields of study. The strength of materials is important for building a bridge, thermodynamics for insulating a home, and aerodynamics for designing an airplane wing. Different principles also apply to institutions in other social spheres. In Figure 7, Appendix, some principles related to each social sphere are shown. The cultural sphere involves values, knowledge, and communication. Economic institutions relate to producing, exchanging, and distributing goods and services. Governance institutions should provide security and regulation.

The previous chapter discusses the principles of consent and checks and balances in legislative institutions. Science and learning are required to design a social institution. Knowledge comes from performance metrics in achieving institutional goals and fixing flaws that cause dysfunction or harm. Just as an individual should seek to produce virtuous actions, a social institution's culture should value ethical behavior. This requires suitable mechanisms of feedback about any harm an institution may cause as a byproduct of its actions.

INDIVIDUAL SOVEREIGNTY AND CONFLICTS OF INTEREST

The most important question to ask in evaluating any social institution is whether it serves the people it is designed to serve or some other purpose.

The primary product of a family is the children it raises into adults. Do they become sovereign individuals, capable of constructive social relationships, economic self-reliance, and good citizenship? Or do they exhibit psychological instability, social or chemical dependency, or destructive behavior? If a society does not produce sovereign individuals, it cannot flourish or sustain existence beyond a feudal society.

Most social institutions assist families in facilitating individual sovereignty in one way or another. Schools provide education and social skills. Clubs like Boy Scouts and 4-H provide economic and citizenship skills. Banks can assist in providing loans if the family can't directly provide financial resources. The government disciplines through law if the family fails to instill self-discipline.

A public school fails its mission to create sovereign individuals if graduates cannot read, write, think critically, have basic health and home-making skills, production skills, business skills, and general knowledge of history and geography. If the school taught things that directly led to the loss of sovereignty, such as encouraging dependency or some form of addiction, it would behave unethically.

We can evaluate any social institution. Does a bank provide a loan with an interest that enables an individual to pay off a home loan with reasonable effort, or does it behave like a loan shark and take advantage of the borrower and keep them in debt slavery? Does a government allow citizens to provide critical feedback on social policy, or does it censor such speech? Whether a social institution supports or hinders individual sovereignty indicates whether it is good or bad.

Conflicts of interest are perhaps the most common structural failure of social institutions. They exist in all social institutions. Most boards require members to declare conflicts of interest and abstain from voting on any issue where there is a conflict. For example, if you are a school board member who owns a vending machine company, you should abstain from the vote on which company will install machines at the school. Any institutional decision affecting whether a person, family member, or interest group, would receive a financial payment is a conflict of interest.

Legislation that does not represent a consensus of the governed would be considered a conflict of interest with the institutional mission. Institutional behavior that conflicts with its mission often hurts individual sovereignty and the general society. Nearly every federal omnibus bill contains earmarks that serve only a few people, a corporation, and NGO, or a city. Congress earmarked $320 million of federal taxpayer dollars for the infamous "bridge to nowhere" that would have replaced the ferry service to an island with 50 residents. Projects that serve a few people do not reflect a consensus of the governed and reveal how the process of creating omnibus legislation is an unethical institutional process designed to produce corrupt results.

Personal conflicts of interest have long been a social concern, but conflicts of interest in institutional processes need to be addressed in an integral society.

Chapter
11

Money and Banking in an Integral Society

The great trouble is that money wasn't allowed to develop. After two or three hundred years of the use of coins, governments stopped any further developments. We were not allowed to experiment on it, so money hasn't been improved, it has rather become worse in the course of time. Menger, and before him Hume and Mandeville, named law, language, and money as the three paradigms of spontaneously occurring institutions. Now fortunately, law and language have been allowed to develop. Money was frozen in its most primitive form. What we have had since was mostly government abuses of money.[1]—F. A. Hayek

The economic sphere has lagged behind the cultural and political spheres in institutional evolution. In the cultural sphere, the Protestant Reformation promoted individual sovereignty, freeing personal belief and thought from the control of the church. Modern liberal democracies responded to demands for personal freedom and sovereignty in the political sphere. In the economic sphere, private property ownership has been established, but the institutions of money creation and banking have not promoted equal opportunity.

The Federal Reserve in the U.S. and the European Central Bank are systems of economic feudalism in which money creators control its

---

1. Friedrich A. Hayek. Interview by James U. Blanchard III, May 1, 1984. Cato Institute Policy Report May/June 1984. https://www.cato.org/policy-report/may/june-1984/exclusive-interview-fa-hayek#.

distribution. In the Dark Ages, feudal lords controlled land distribution. New money distribution is a form of economic injustice not widely understood and referred to as a secret or mystery.[2] This economic injustice cannot exist in an integral society. Economic sovereignty needs to catch up with evolving cultural and political sovereignty.

Economic injustice is opposed by churches, Marxists, and movements like Occupy Wall Street. There are many slogans calling for the end of "capitalism" or "corporate greed" based on the effects of economic injustice. However, these are reactions to economic injustice without a functional vision of financial institutions that promote personal economic sovereignty. People calling for state-planned economies and taxing the rich appear oblivious to the injustices of government/bank intrigues that are the source of injustice.

This chapter provides a brief overview of the nature of money and banking and argues that government debt-financed money creation is a strategy of collusion that redirects money from the hard work of citizens and taxpayers to wealthy elites. Then a case is made for the wide distribution of new money and ownership of capital.

MONEY

Money existed in prehistoric times. As Frederick Hayek stated, it is a spontaneously occurring social institution. Even hunter-gather societies traded among themselves. Barter was commonplace, but some societies used shells, beads, whale teeth, or even stone disks as money.[3] Alan Meltzer described money as follows:

> **Money,** a commodity accepted by general consent as a medium of economic exchange. It is the medium in which prices and values are expressed; as currency, it circulates anonymously from person to person

2. Murray N. Rothbard, *The Mystery of Banking,* Second ed. (Auburn AL: Ludwig von Mises Institute, 1983).

3. Alan H. Meltzer, "Money," *Britannica.com* https://www.britannica.com/topic/money

and country to country, thus facilitating trade, and it is the principal measure of wealth.[4]

Money represents a value of exchange. It is only as good as the faith people have in it. Money can be an agreement between two parties, as in a promissory note. A seller or lender must believe that the borrower will pay over time. Money can be a society's standardized medium of exchange, for example, beads, pieces of metal, coins, paper notes, and now cryptocurrencies.

Currency is as good as its value to the people who exchange it. It is most widely accepted and trusted when it is stable over time. In early Western civilization, the currency had intrinsic value, like grain, blobs of gold or silver, or metal coins. Gold could be turned into jewelry or iron into tools. Paper notes, which have no intrinsic value, were initially backed by assets like gold and silver and could be redeemed for these assets.

Fiat currency has no intrinsic value and cannot be exchanged for assets. It is an official unit of exchange decreed by a government. Fiat currency only works when people have faith in it. This requires the government to prevent inflation and protection against counterfeiting that would increase the money supply.[5] If a fiat currency is not managed well, people will abandon its use and seek other ways of economic exchange. Despite widespread criticism, fiat currency has been used successfully and stimulated economic growth when well-managed. However, mismanagement of fiat currency causes entire economies to collapse and the widespread suffering of people, causing opposition to its use.

FRAUD AND THE DEBASING OF MONEY

Fraud is the misrepresentation of the value of what someone is receiving for their money. The promise of money is a great temptation for the abuse of trust by individuals and social institutions. There are well-established

---

4. Ibid.

5. "Fiat Money," Corporate Finance Institute. https://corporatefinanceinstitute. com/resources/knowledge/economics/fiat-money-currency/.

laws against fraud committed by individuals, such as embezzlement, mail fraud, investment fraud, and fraudulent advertising.

In ancient times currency fraud occurred by rigging scales, showing a false weight and value of gold or silver. Early laws in Babylon penalized these types of fraud. Lydia's King Alyattes stepped in to regulate coinage about 600 B.C. by minting the stater. Rulers put a stamp on coins after they authenticated its weight and content.

But after governments began minting coins, new ways to commit fraud developed. Governments could debase the value of metal coins by diluting the percentage of the precious metal in the object and falsely authenticating it. Individuals tried to abuse government coins by shaving the weight and melting the shavings, and counterfeiting arose.

Today governments are used for committing fraud by borrowing money for expenses that do not represent the consent of the taxpayers who . are on the hook for this debt. Omnibus legislation is a way such fraud is committed. Fraud is also committed in the misuse of public money by members of government agencies who spend without a consciousness that they have a sacred duty to use public money ethically or not correctly using government grants or research money. Classifying documents is a way to hide misspent money.

How can a government be a referee or authenticator of money if it spends money it creates? That is a conflict of interest. In the United States, the state governments cannot print money to pay off loans They have to balance their budgets and not cause inflation. However, the U.S. Federal Reserve, the Bank of England, and the European Central Bank print money for governments to cover the previous debt, placing unlimited burdens on taxpayers and future generations for bureaucratic and military expenditures. The recipients of this new money earn higher wages than those paying the taxes. This is a form of exploitation and structural injustice.

Who guards the guardian? Marxism is not a solution; it makes the government a player rather than a referee. The solution is to prevent the government from being a player and it's access to new money through government/bank cabals.

GOVERNMENT AS ECONOMIC REFEREE, NOT PLAYER

Some governments are good economic referees. The ancient Greek *drachma* contained 67 grams of silver from Solon (594 B.C.) to Alexander and 65 grains afterward. When other governments fiddled with their coins, the drachma became widely used in Asia and Europe well into the 2nd-century A.D.[6] This stable currency with intrinsic value aided the rise of the Greek economy and the spread of Greek civilization.

Rome introduced its currency introduced in 87 B.C. It remained uncorrupted until the time of Nero in 54 A.D. The debasing of money was slight at the beginning and had little impact on society through the reign of the Five Good Emperors. Between the third and fifth centuries A.D., currency debasement contributed to the destruction of the middle-class and the Empire (see Chapter 3).

In the twentieth century, there has been inflation with government-printed fiat currencies. In the U.S., gold went up ten times from $35 per ounce in 1971 to $350 per ounce in 2002. That is an average of 7.5% inflation over 30 years. Hyperinflation is inflation that spirals out of control when governments try to print their way out of money mismanagement. Here is what happened in the Weimar Republic:

> One dozen eggs cost a half-Reichsmark in 1918 and three Reichsmarks in 1921. In 1923, the market price increased to 500 (January) then 30 million (September) and four billion Reichsmarks (October)....
>
> Before World War I, one US dollar had purchased about four Reichsmarks.... At the worst of the hyperinflation in late 1923, the exchange rate for one US dollar had skyrocketed to 48,000 Reichsmarks (January) then 192,000 (June) 170 billion (October) and four trillion (November).[7]

More recently, Venezuela's hyperinflation reached 10 million percent in 2018. The oil-rich country was bankrupt because its money was worth

---

6. Meltzer, "Money," *op. cit.*

7. Jennifer Llewellyn, Steve Thompson, "The hyperinflation of 1923," Alpha History, September 26, 2019. https://alphahistory.com/weimarrepublic/1923-hyperinflation/.

practically nothing, and its economy was producing almost nothing, forcing people to barter or trade in other currencies. The flow of money follows natural principles that governments cannot change by force. Governments can referee exchanges, but can't produce more goods and services people want by printing money. Only a well-refereed economy that gives citizens economic sovereignty can do that.

When the government acts as a referee and protects the stability of money, the economy can grow, and the people prosper. However, when government becomes a player and uses its monopoly power to create debased money for the elite, it destroys the economy and the lives of the productive citizens.

BANKS OF DEPOSIT, EXCHANGE, AND LENDING

Banks are fundamental financial institutions that store or exchange money. The earliest form of banking was charging a storage fee for the safekeeping of gold or other assets. These are called *banks of deposit.* They stored money or precious objects in a vault until the owner wanted it back. Banks could not use this money for lending or speculation because it was not theirs.

Lending money began as a separate business. A moneylender would lend his own money, which the borrower would repay with agreed-upon interest. However, bankers sitting on quantities of money that belong to someone else are always tempted to lend or invest it as if it was theirs. In the Middle Ages, when modern banking was born in Italy, some bankers used a portion of the money they were storing for depositors for lending or other investments, assuming they would have enough reserves to pay when requested. But when the banks got caught cheating, depositors would make a run on the bank to withdraw their deposits and cause bankruptcy.

The Venetian government initially got involved as a referee to stop this behavior. In 1361, the Senate passed a law prohibiting banks from misusing deposits. But many bankers ignored the law, outspent reserves, and went bankrupt. The next step was for the government, in 1524, to create a board of bank examiners to inspect banks to ensure all deposits remained in storage. Bank examiners must have been tempted by bribes from bankers, for in 1584, the largest bank in Italy, the house of Pisano and Tiepolo, failed when it could not pay depositors from reserves.

Next, the government set up a state bank, the *Banco Della Piazza del Rialto,* that was not allowed to make loans. The bank was only allowed to earn money from fees for services: coin storage, currency exchange fees, transfers of payments between customers, and notary signatures.[8] This was honest banking. The paper notes issued by the *Banco Della Piazza del Rialto* became more valuable than coins because they were more dependable than money with unknown levels of purity.

Functional and stable deposit banking was established. The state had set up the *Banco Della Piazza del Rialto,* primarily as a referee that earned no profit from it. The laws regarding the bank treated individual depositors as sovereigns, as an integral society requires. While people trusted this bank, it was eventually replaced by other banks that engaged in lending from reserves. As long as lending was modest, banks survived, but there was always a possibility of collapse.

In 1609 the Bank of Amsterdam was created as an *exchange bank.* The small country was awash in coins and currencies from various issuers. Some coins were debased, and it was hard for merchants to know what coins were worth. Merchants want a place to settle payments in foreign currencies safely. The Bank of Amsterdam brokered the exchange of money and guaranteed the settlements in an accounting unit called the *florin.* The charter of the bank forbade lending.

The florin was the first instance of what is now called *stablecoin.*[9] It was an exchange unit for business transactions. It was based on the different currencies' gold and silver asset value. Stablecoin is a recent term developed to describe cryptocurrencies whose value is pegged to some

---

8. John Kenneth Galbraith, *Money: Whence It Came, Where It Went* (Princeton University Press, 2017, first published 1976), p. 19.

9. Jon Frost, Hyun Song Shin and Peter Wierts, "An early stablecoin? The Bank of Amsterdam and the governance of money." BIS Working Papers, No 902, November 2020.

outside reference, either hard assets or stable fiat money like the dollar, to maintain price stability for commercial transactions.

The City Council chartered the Bank of Amsterdam was chartered to perform the job of a monetary referee. The bank formed a single economic function that escaped many government conflicts of interest. The separation of the economic and government spheres made it an integral institution whose mission was the reliable exchange of money.

This bank emerged as the first *central bank:*

> By the end of the seventeenth century, the Bank of Amsterdam was performing three functions that are routinely carried out by central banks today: operating a large-value payment system, creating a form of money not directly redeemable for coin, and managing the value of this money through open market operations.[10]

Due to its sound financial practices, the Bank of Amsterdam's currency became a reserve currency, the dominant currency in Europe in the 17th and 18th centuries.[11] The bank eventually lost that status after abandoning its mission. As had been the case in Venice, the bank finally succumbed to temptation, first allowing depositors to overdraw their accounts and later secretly lending to the Dutch East India Company, which ran up massive debt in 1779 that it could not repay. Depositors lost trust, and a bank run made it technically insolvent.[12]

The lesson provided by the history of the Bank of Amsterdam is that it succeeded as a central bank when it was a referee and not a player. It accomplished what no central bank has done since, acting strictly as a referee. Stephen Quinn and William Roberds argue the Bank of Amsterdam avoided two questionable functions of modern central banks:

10. Stephen Quinn and William Roberds, "An Economic Explanation of the Early Bank of Amsterdam, Debasement, Bills of Exchange, and the Emergence of the First Central Bank," Federal Reserve Bank of Atlanta, Working Paper 2006-13. September 2006. https://www.atlantafed.org/research/publications/wp/2006/13.

11. Stephen Quinn and William Roberds, "Death of a Reserve Currency," *International Journal of Central Banking,* December 2016, pp. 63-103.

12. This was not a complete insolvency, but a policy insolvency, because it carried more debt than reserves.

Ironically, the Bank of Amsterdam may be best remembered for what it did not do, i.e., take on what are now viewed as the definitive central-bank functions of circulating note issue, operation of a discount window, and the purchase of government securities.[13]

Honest financial services of storing, lending, and exchanging currency do not involve new money creation through fractional reserve banking.

FRACTIONAL RESERVE BANKING AND ABUSE

Fractional reserve banking refers to a policy that requires banks to keep a fraction of their deposits "in reserve" rather than retaining them all in storage when creating a loan. The rationale for allowing this is that not every depositor will withdraw all deposits simultaneously. Keeping enough reserve to meet the withdrawal demand enables the bank to lend out more money than exists, creating new money when the loan is repaid. This new money creation allows an economy to expand and people to start new businesses.

In the Middle Ages, fractional reserve banking was illegal and considered cheating or theft because the bank's used other people's stored deposits. Fractional reserve banking as we know it today began in 1668 with the Riksbank in Sweden and quickly expanded to other central banks, including the United States, in 1791.[14] Today fractional reserve banking is a standard practice around the world. This is explained by Harold G. Moulton in his 1935 book, *Income and Economic Progress:*

> A new and even more dynamic factor has come into the process of capital formation through the evolution of modern commercial banking. The development of the banking system, with its ability to manufacture credit, has served to render funds immediately available for the purposes of capital creation without the necessity of waiting upon the slower processes of accumulating funds from individual savings. The

---

13. Stephen Quinn and William Roberds, "An Economic Explanation... .," *op. cit.*

14. "A simple guide to fractional reserve banking," CORO. https://coro.global/blog/a-simple-guide-to-fractional-reserve-banking/

result is to sustain productivity at a higher level and to facilitate the growth of new capital at a more rapid rate than would otherwise have occurred.[15]

However, fractional reserve lending is practiced unethically because the principal payments on the loans go to the banks and not the depositors whose assets back the loans. This process would be ethical if the income from the fractional reserve lending went to the depositors. Banks should be allowed to take interest on the loan as a service fee for originating and maintaining it.

I will use an example to make the problem clear.

Imagine you have $100,000 in a savings account. The bank lends out $900,000, keeping $100,000, the required 10% reserve. When that loan is repaid, you should get the $900,000, making your account balance $1 million. If this is a typical 5-year business loan, you have earned 180% per year! If this is a 30-year mortgage, you will be making 30% per year!

The borrower usually pays the loan insurance fee, so you don't have to worry about risk. Further, the interest on the loan will more than cover the bank's service fee, which would be the bank employee's labor income. In the above example, if the loan was 8%, the interest on a small business loan today, there would be $194,925.29 paid in interest. If it was a 30-year home loan for that amount paid 5% interest, the interest would be $839,302.06, more than enough for the bank to administer the loan.[16]

This sounds too good to be true, but this is what the bankers are taking home today using fractional reserve lending. The amount of new money created on shorter loans is the same, so the return percentage is considerable. Commercial banks can earn money many times faster than community banks specializing in home mortgages. That money should go to the investors, who are ordinary working people with savings accounts.

15. Harold G. Moulton, *Income and Economic Progress* (Washington, DC: The Brookings Institution, 1935), p. 5.

16. Example mine.

The current lending process enables banks to receive an estimated 97 percent of the new money.[17] This creates an ever-expanding wealth gap. They are taking money that rightfully belongs to the savers. If the people with savings accounts received these new money loan principal payments, capital would be widely distributed, and there would be a large middle class with economic autonomy to support a republican form of democracy.

Fractional reserve banking has proven to be a safe method for expanding an economy when statistically sound reserve requirements are met and when loan insurance or collateral protects the investors in the case of loan failure.

Loans, by nature, are a form of economic serfdom. They provide a means for individuals without capital to gain economic autonomy over time. This practice can be seen as a variation on indentured servitude that enables immigrants to earn their economic freedom. People are willing to borrow from banks or work as indentured servants if it means future financial independence. This is a method of enabling upward economic mobility that societies need to prosper.

BANK SPECULATION

Abuse of society by financial institutions is not limited to theft from the holders of savings accounts through fractional reserve lending. That makes the rich richer, but doesn't put the economic system at risk. New money needs to go for real production of goods and economic expansion. But much of the lending and investment money goes for speculative and non-productive purposes.

New money gets used for risky stock speculation, secondary financial paper like sub-prime mortgages and derivatives, and government borrowing for bureaucratic expansion and military arms. These activities do not produce assets representing economic growth. Instead, they lead to inflation and economic collapse. Bank speculation contributed to the

---

17. See, *97 % Owned,* a documentary on this problem. http://97percentowned. com/press/

stock market bubble that collapsed in 1929. Excessive belief in the stock market created fast money in the roaring 20s as businesses and the economy rapidly expanded. Banks speculating with depositors' money greatly inflated the bubble. Bank failures followed the stock market collapse. Gambling with depositor money is far riskier than lending from reserves.

The government stepped in as a referee to stop unethical bank speculation. The Glass-Steagall Act of 1933 corrected two serious problems. First, it prohibited banks from using deposits for speculation rather than traditional secure lending practices. Second, it established the FDIC to protect sovereign citizens from institutional malfeasance if the banks did fail. The Glass-Steagall Act was one of the best pieces of financial legislation in U.S. history. Unfortunately, it was repealed in 1999 and immediately followed by unethical practices and scandals like Enron and WorldCom and then the 2008 financial crisis.

A new form of bank abuse emerged. Adopting an "originate to distribute" model of bank lending introduced new risks into the financial system.[18] If a bank originates a loan and immediately resells it to investors, it takes a profit off the top and passes all loan risks to the buyers. Traditionally, a bank holds the loan it issues, so it is careful to originate a sound loan. However, if a bank can resell its loans to investors in secondary markets, it will be motivated to make as many risky loans as possible and let others take the risk. This practice dramatically increased after the Glass-Steagall Act was repealed:

> In 1993, all together, non-bank investors acquired 13.2 percent of the term loans originated that year. In 2007, they acquired 56.3 percent of the term loans originated in that year, a 327 percentage point increase from fifteen years earlier.[19]

Many economists argue that banks must hold the loans they originate

---

18. Vitaly M. Bord and João A. C. Santos, "The Rise of the Originate-to-Distribute Model and the Role of Banks in Financial Intermediation," RBNY Economic Policy Review / July 2012, pp. 21-34.

19. Ibid., p. 22.

to maturity and not sell in secondary markets.[20] Banks must take responsibility for the loans they originate.

The secondary financial market activities of loan bundling, syndication, derivatives, and insurance were not even well-understood by the investment companies that bought them. The risky loans created a housing bubble followed by foreclosures and the housing market crash of 2007. The unethical lending practices hurt thousands of homeowners and investors, depriving them of personal economic sovereignty. The government failed to act as a referee as it had done in 1933. Instead, it bailed out the institutions that had harmed society and passed laws the bog banks proposed, making them more powerful. Small community banks, best suited to monitor the loans they originate, disappeared.

The obvious solution would have been to reign in the banks by reimposing the Glass-Steagall Act as former Federal Reserve Chairman Paul Volker recommended:

> The *New York Times* today has an article about former Federal Reserve Chairman Paul Volcker's crusade to bring back the Glass-Steagall Act. Obama isn't listening. The Act used to keep separate commercial and investment banking activities. The Gramm-Leach-Bliley Act of 1999 repealed it. Consequently "full service" banking behemoths like Citigroup and JP Morgan came to be, now allowed to participate in every financial activity imaginable. Many, including Volcker, believe this was a big mistake, and one of the causes of the financial crisis. *I don't see it. At all.*[21]

The above quote from *The Atlantic* was written as a defense of the banks. Corporate-owned media, like the *Atlantic,* promoted hollow legislation like the Sarbanes-Oxley Act and the Dodd-Frank Act, drafted by the financial institutions that owned them. These acts were unethical legislation that enabled the most politically influential financial firms to prosper at the expense of the more productive and ethical small firms.

On the right, several politicians like Ron Paul argued to "end the

---

20. Ibid. pp. 22-23.
21. *The Atlantic,* October 21, 2009. Italics mine.

Fed" or return to the gold standard. Those on the left got behind the Occupy Wall Street Movement to "tax the rich," staging a sit-in around Zuccotti Park in lower Manhattan on September 17, 2011.[22] The problems were not fixed but got worse. The banks continued to print money, trade derivatives, credit swaps, adjustable-rate mortgages, and other risky investments. They managed to avoid inflation by driving interest rates to zero, further harming small banks. The working-class savings accounts that should earn 30 percent or more in an honest lending system, saw a less than one percent return on their savings.

Further, reserve rates were raised after the big banks received a federal injection of cash. Small banks that did nothing to cause the meltdown didn't have these reserves. They were forced many out of business or taken over by the large banks. Dodd-Frank regulation made it difficult for new banks to start up. Ellen Brown observed that by 2014,

> The number of small banks in the U.S. ha(d) shrunk by 9.5% just since the Dodd-Frank Act was passed in 2010, and their share of U.S. banking assets ha(d) shrunk by 18.6%.[23]

In March 2020, the Federal Reserve reduced the reserve rate on the big banks to zero, putting the entire system at greater risk. Congress approved trillions in government loans that fed a government-bank cabal ready to collapse.

GOVERNMENT-BANK CABALS

Governments learned the tremendous amount of cash that fractional reserve lending can generate. They saw how the bankers could get rich through taking the principal payments on the new money and wanted in on the action. The arrangement normally goes like this:

---

22. "Occupy Wall Street Begins," *History .com*. https://www.history.com/this-day-in-history/occupy-wall-street-begins-zuccotti-park

23. Ellen Brown, "Why Do Banks Want Our Deposits? Hint: It's Not to Make Loans," The *Web of Deby Blog*. Oct. 26, 2014. https://ellenbrown.com/2014/10/26/why-do-banks-want-our-deposits-hint-its-not-to-make-loans/

We, the government Parliament or Senate, know that you, the banks, are profiting immensely through fractional reserve lending that does not return the new money to the people whose savings has generated it. We have the power to shut you down or conduct honest banking, but will look the other way if we can get in on the action.

Here is what we'll do. We will allow you to continue if you loan to us all the new money we ask for. We can use this for a military that will protect you. This debt will be guaranteed though taxes on the people and inflation. You will remit excess earnings to the Treasury after providing for operating expenses, payment of dividends, and the amount necessary to maintain surplus.[24]

In this type of cabal the new money created by largely nonproductive government debt is divided between the bank and the treasury. The process is shrouded in mystery.[25] This type of cabal robs citizens of their economic sovereignty.

The Bank of England, chartered in 1694, was the first modern government-bank cabal. King William needed money for war, but the government, unable to increase taxes or borrow, became desperate for another way to obtain money. Parliament gave the new Bank of England the advantage of holding all government deposits, as well as the power to issue new notes to pay for the government debt. Murray Rothbard describes what followed:

> The Bank of England promptly issued the enormous sum of £760,000, most of which was used to buy government debt. This had an immediate and considerable inflationary effect, and in the short span of two years, the Bank of England was insolvent after a bank run, an insolvency gleefully abetted by its competitors, the private goldsmiths, who were happy to return to it the swollen Bank of England notes for redemption in specie.

---

24. The narrative is mine, but the final sentence is from a U.S. Federal Reserve publicity release in 2022. https://www.federalreserve.gov/newsevents/pressreleases/other20220114a.htm

25. Murray N. Rothbard, *The Mystery of Banking,* Second ed. (Auburn AL: Ludwig von Mises Institute, 1983).

It was at this point that a fateful decision was made, one which set a grave and mischievous precedent for both British and American banking. In May 1696, the English government simply allowed the Bank of England to "suspend specie payment"—that is, to refuse to pay its contractual obligations of redeeming its notes in gold—yet to continue in operation, issuing notes and enforcing payments upon its own debtors. The Bank of England suspended specie payment, and its notes promptly fell to a 20 percent discount against specie, since no one knew if the Bank would ever resume payment in gold.

The straits of the Bank of England were shown in an account submitted at the end of 1696, when its notes outstanding were £765,000, backed by only £36,000 in cash. In those days, few note holders were willing to sit still and hold notes when there was such a low fraction of cash.

Specie payments resumed two years later, but the rest of the early history of the Bank of England was a shameful record of periodic suspensions of specie payment, despite an ever-increasing set of special privileges conferred upon it by the British government.[26]

The Bank of England was the first bank declared "too big to fail." The bank created fiat money and earned eight percent interest on loans to the government. The government received easy access to this money to finance wars and other political agendas without an upfront tax on citizens. The bank convinced the government to abandon new bank charters, declare notes from the Bank of England the only legal tender, and pass a law that put counterfeiters to death. Only a cartel with government protection can enjoy such insulation from the workings of a free market in money.[27] The pattern of government-central bank cabal was established and has become widespread.

The U.S. was divided over implementing such a legalized cabal. Alexander Hamilton argued for it, and Thomas Jefferson opposed it. Hamilton's model eventually won. Banks were not well-regulated and frequently failed, causing panic and financial ruin for citizens. In the 1830s, Andrew Jackson advocated the separation of banking and the

26. Murray N. Rothbard, *The Mystery of Banking,* p. 180.
27. Ibid.

state. Banking was centralized during the Civil War and was followed by several inflations and recessions.

In an integral society, the government needs to referee banks. The absolute separation of banks from the state, free banks,[28] allows banks to fail and leaves consumers at their peril. It does not protect personal economic sovereignty. The opposite extreme is when the government is a player, profiting from a new money cabal where elites appropriate most of the wealth.

The U.S. Federal Reserve Act of 1913, modeled on the British system, introduced a private central bank in which the government was the primary player, not a referee. The government immediately used the system to create debt to fund the First World War.

The U.S. Constitution had to be changed to establish the Federal Reserve. The Constitution forbade the direct taxation of citizens and required all taxes to be apportioned.[29] The 16th Amendment was necessary to tax citizens directly to finance the loans. The state governments were bypassed, violating the principle of subsidiarity.

The Federal Reserve could purchase government debt with money created out of thin air. The U.S. Congress abandoned its responsibility to balance the budget, as individuals and other institutions must do, and just increased the debt. Politicians unable to control their spending had a new means to fund lobbyists and political parties. Deprived of economic sovereignty, citizens were forced to pay unwanted expenses through inflation. Economist John Maynard Keynes described this shifted wealth from the masses to elites:

> By a continuing process of inflation, governments can confiscate, secretly and unobserved, an important part of the wealth of their citizens. By this method they not only confiscate, but they confiscate arbitrarily; and, while the process impoverishes many, it actually enriches

---

28. Rothbard, *The Mystery of Banking*, p. 215.

29. The Constitution, Article I, section 9, clause 4. "No Capitation, or other direct, Tax shall be laid, unless in Proportion to the Census or enumeration herein before directed to be taken."

some. The sight of this arbitrary rearrangement of riches strikes not only at security, but at confidence in the equity of the existing distribution of wealth.[30]

The Federal Reserve has no incentive to reduce government debt and the hidden costs of inflation. It describes its mission as:

> The goals of monetary policy are to promote maximum employment, stable prices and moderate long-term interest rates. By implementing effective monetary policy, the Fed can maintain stable prices, thereby supporting conditions for long-term economic growth and maximum employment.[31]

After the Dodd-Frank legislation of 2010, the complexity of the cabal increased. Banks are allowed to borrow from the Fed short-term loans at close to zero percent interest, and they can use this money to buy Treasury Bonds and mortgage-backed bonds in the secondary market. Banks can then sit back and earn money on this interest differential without needed deposits or lending:

> Lending is no longer the banks' core activity. Instead, banks make most of their income from trading—for example, in 2010, the six largest bank holding companies generated 74 percent of their pretax income from trading (Wilmers 2011) and yield-curve riding courtesy of the Fed.

> The Fed's interest rate policy allows banks to borrow short-term at close to zero and invest at around 3 percent in long-term Treasuries and even more in mortgage-backed bonds, which are now openly guaranteed by the federal government. This enables them to sit back with 3 percent spreads leveraged 15 times or so to make a comfortable 45 percent or more return. Becoming a yield curve player is far more profitable and avoids all that tiresome bother and risk of lending to small businesses.[32]

---

30. John Maynard Keynes, *The Economic Consequences of the Peace*, Chapter 5. http://www.gutenberg.org/etext/15776

31. Federal Reserve Eductaion.org https://www.federalreserveeducation.org/about-the-fed/structure-and-functions/monetary-policy

32. Kevin Dowd, Martin Hutchinson, and Gordon Kerr "The Coming Fiat Money Cataclysm and the Case for Gold" *Cato Journal*, Vol. 32, No. 2 (Spring/Summer 2012).

Governments are non-productive institutions, and banks as "yield curve players," also become non-productive institutions. The new non-productive fiat money produced governments and bank cabals, causing inflation borne by citizens doing the productive work. The producers work, and the non-producers get the money.

This system creates an inflationary bubble followed by an economic recession. Government debt-produced fiat money is the core problem, not the idea of fiat money itself. Restraints on government debt are necessary, but there are no institutional restraints on either banks or the government.

A more integral economic system would, like the Glass-Steagall Act, limit government and economic institutions to specific missions designed to serve the citizens. It is a conflict of interest for a government to borrow money it can print. The type of bank cabal that began in England more than three hundred years ago and spread throughout the world needs to end. Governments should directly borrow from their citizens or independent institutions. A central bank can act as a clearing house, but it should not be allowed to fund government debt.

Stabilizing Money

Fiat currency can be stable if it is regulated well and trusted. Bank notes were traditionally backed by gold and silver, but the value of precious metals also fluctuates based on supply and demand. Economist David Ricardo proposed the best fix for an inflationary fiat system was to require money to be backed by some type of asset. While gold and silver are not perfect money assets, he stated: "They are, however, the best with which we are acquainted."[33] Throughout the 19th century, British and American governments created an official price of gold at £4.25 and approximately $20[34] for an ounce, respectively. Their notes were redeem-

---

33. David Ricardo, *The Works and Correspondence of David Ricardo: Pamphlets 1815- 1823,* Piero Sraffa, ed. (Cambridge: Cambridge University Press, 1951), Vol. IV, p.58-62.

34. From 1791-1833, gold was $19.39 and from 1834-1933 $20. In 1933 U.S. President Roosevelt demanded citizens turn in all gold and then reset the price to $35 per ounce in 1934. Citizens were not allowed to own gold until 1974.

able in gold. International trade flourished when gold backed many
national currencies, causing global monetary stability. After World War
I, many countries had to adjust the value of their money.

The Bretton Woods Agreement after World War II tied all currencies
to the dollar and the dollar to gold at $35 per ounce. The U.S. held the
world's largest reserves of gold, and the dollar became the world reserve
currency. U.S. gold reserves dwindled to less than half their post-war
amount by 1971. President Nixon took the U.S. off of the gold standard,
and paper currency was all that backed the "world reserve currency" after
that.

Trading of world petroleum in dollars, the "petrodollar," added some
stability to the dollar after the gold standard was abandoned. Energy is
required for most production and correlates more closely to economic
growth than gold. One alternative proposal is tying money to energy.[35]
Economists are also devising other formulas that describe economic
growth, many of which include GDP as a factor. Governments and central banks resist such procedures because they have become addicted to
the cabals providing "funny money"[36] to elites.

The hegemony of the U.S. dollar ended in 2022. Excessive printing
of COVID-19 relief money not tied to production caused inflation
and loss of confidence in the dollar. Then during the Russia-Ukraine
war, Western sanctions on Russia and other countries stimulated a new
reserve currency created by Russia, China, Brazil, and others.[37] Oil and
other international commodities began trading in Russian Rubles and
other currencies.

---

35. https://energybackedmoney.com/

   https://www.bu.edu/synapse/2009/04/27/powering-up-the-economy/
36. The term "funny money" is defined a artificially inflated currency, or counterfeit
money. It is used to describe the effect of these cabals. https://www.merriam-webster.
com/dictionary/funny%20money
37. Jamie Redman, "Targeting the U.S. Dollar's Hegemony: Russia, China, and
BRICS Nations Plan to Craft a New International Reserve Currency," *Bitcoin.com*.
https://news.bitcoin.com/targeting-the-us-dollars-hegemony-russia-china-and-brics-
nations-plan-to-craft-a-new-international-reserve-currency/

Cryptocurrencies like Bitcoin were created to avoid government malfeasance and make money reliable. However, the experimental nature of cryptocurrency has led to wide swings in value. So far, attempts to create stable cryptocurrencies or stablecoin have been unsatisfactory because they get tied to the dollar and don't escape government manipulation. Central banks are looking at ways to continue government/bank cabals with their digital currencies, eliminating fiat paper money.

Honest Money and Banking in an Integral Society

Honest money and honest banking mean no theft, direct or indirect, shrouded in mystery. Honoring ownership of money is essential for any economy and "Thou shalt not steal" is a foundational principle of civilization and individual economic sovereignty. Fractional reserve banking, as currently practiced, is a form of theft. However, fractional reserve banking could be honest if the principal payments went to everyone's savings accounts.

Creating "new money" that concentrates wealth in the hands of a few elites while imposing a hidden tax on the masses through inflation is unethical. The working class gets exploited twice: first when they are deprived of the increased capital based on their savings accounts, and secondly when they are put on the hook for government debt., Modern government-bank cabals continue this theft in a shroud of secrecy. Ill-gotten gains are used to fund wars and line the pockets of cronies, shackling ordinary citizens.

On the left, socialists and communists voice opposition to the "capitalist system" through movements like Occupy Wall Street. However, their proposals to make government the sole player will create serfdom with new elites in charge.[38] That is substituting one cabal for another. But the current form of capitalism is not the answer either; it is a corrupt cabal. On the right, this system is attacked by economists like Frederick Hayek and Murray Rothbard. Senator Ron Paul's movement advocates "End the Fed" and returning to the gold standard. The solution requires

---

38. F. A. Hayek, *The Road the Serfdom,* Chicago: University of Chicago Press, 1944.

laws that forbid government/bank debt cabals and foster widespread ownership of capital and the economic autonomy of citizens.

An integral society requires changes in the system that keeps banks in a role of serving sovereign individuals and not social institutions. We have proposed dividing principal payments on all loans received by banks to the bank depositors. Banks should be allowed to charge interest for their services of originating and maintaining loans. This would be like honest banking in the late Medieval period, where the role of banks was limited to receiving fees in exchange for services provided.

The ownership of capital needs to be widespread with all people having equal access to the system. We have discussed equal access to new capital through savings accounts. However, production of goods and services also relies on old money in another form of asset, corporate stocks. Corporate stocks represent actual the ownership of the means of production, Marxists have complained about workers not owning the means of production, but they never suggested a way for this to happen. Instead every communist system has prevented workers from owning the means of production and handed ownership to party/state cabals that deprive citizens of economic sovereignty more than bank/state cabals.

Ethical ways to reform capitalism so that there is widespread ownership of the means of production are discussed in the next chapter.

Chapter
_12_

Distributing the Ownership of Capital

New estimates show that just eight men own the same wealth as the poorest half of the world. As growth benefits the richest, the rest of society—especially the poorest—suffers. The very design of our economies and the principles of our economics have taken us to this extreme, unsustainable, and unjust point.[1]

CAPITAL CONCENTRATION AND ECONOMIC FEUDALISM

The individual ownership of farms, businesses, and industries in the West has been steadily displaced by consolidated ownership of resources and production by wealthy individuals and financial institutions. We have shown how current banking practices and cabals aid this capital concentration. This consolidation is not economic democracy but a path to economic feudalism. How can ownership of capital become more widespread in an integral society that does not allow theft>

In the last chapter, we traced the origin of this problem to the Bank of England's bailout by Parliament in 1696. This has become an unethical form of capitalism practiced all over the world. The results of this unjust economic system were harshly criticized by Karl Marx and Frederick Engels, who named this system "capitalism." Marx was frustrated that

---

1. Deborah Hardoon, "An economy for the 99%: It's time to build a human economy that benefits everyone, not just the privileged few," Oxfam International Policy Paper, 16 January 2017,

large corporations using machine labor created "surplus populations" without work and income. The owners of capital were getting wealthy while the surplus labor drove wages to a subsistence level under oppressive working conditions.

Marx compared this economic serfdom in industrial society to the agricultural serfdom in a feudal society, where land ownership was concentrated in the hands of a few feudal lords. He called this system "bourgeois property" ownership. Economic feudalism might be another term. Marx explained his concept of "property" in nuanced terms:

> The French Revolution, for example, abolished feudal property in favour of bourgeois property. The distinguishing feature of Communism is not the abolition of property generally, but the abolition of bourgeois property. But modern bourgeois private property is the final and most complete expression of the system of producing and appropriating products, that is based on class antagonisms, on the exploitation of the many by the few.
>
> In this sense, the theory of the Communists may be summed up in the single sentence: Abolition of private property.[2]

In the above paragraphs, the terms "feudal property," "bourgeois property," and "private property" mean specific things. Feudal property is land ownership by kings, princes, and the church in an agrarian economy. There is no method of capital-based development or innovation in such an economy. Bourgeois property is based on wealthy elite ownership of the means of industrial production of goods—factories that require large amounts of capital not available to workers.

"Private property," for Marx, was not what individuals own for daily living but "bourgeois private property," or capital, that was used by the wealthy class to enslave the typical worker. The control system of capital—the factories, banks, money, laws, and natural resources—was in the

---

2. Karl Marx and Frederick Engels, *The Communist Manifesto,* Chapter 2, 1848. https://www.marxists.org/archive/marx/works/1848/communist-manifesto/ch02.htm

hands of a few. Marx's solution was not the distribution of the ownership of capital to sovereign individuals but to "collective ownership":

> Capital is therefore not only personal; it is a social power.
>
> When, therefore, capital is converted into common property, into the property of all members of society, personal property is not thereby transformed into social property. It is only the social character of the property that is changed. It loses its class character.[3]

The core problem of Marxism lays in the concept of "collective property." It is not owned by sovereign citizens, but a social institution claiming to act on their behalf. In practice, this is ownership by the state or the Communist Party, which are government entities. Such ownership prevents individual economic sovereignty and misallocates resources.

Marxist naive faith in government and social institutions always leads to catastrophic results. There are no checks and balances, and the government is an economic player rather than a referee. The state will inevitably violate individual rights for its own interest. Governments, by nature, are unproductive monopolies. Financial incentive and productivity stem from the spontaneous human to produce and exchange. Marxism suppress this natural human desire.

Marxism is an influential critique of the current economic system, which is why its appeal to idealistic young people continues, despite actual failure in practice. People are not motivated to work for others' goals or visions of "collective good." They want to control their own lives and financial destiny. Economic sovereignty is not only ownership of personal things but also the labor and capital that enable personal economic autonomy. Ownership should neither be concentrated in the hands of "bourgeois" elites or some government but distributed among sovereign individuals without theft or violence.

In the Soviet Union and in China, before the reforms under Deng Xiaoping,[4] the communist economy was state feudalism. Deng's reforms

---

3. Ibid.
4. "Deng Xiaoping," *Encyclopedia Brittanica,* https://www.britannica.com/biography/Deng-Xiaoping

(1978-1985) recognized the necessity of individual economic sovereignty and decentralization for improved economic productivity. China's economic reforms moved towards the government acting as a referee. This sparked dramatic growth in the Chinese economy. However, China's economy still resembles a "bourgeois" economy with government-bank cabals and party members on corporate boards. Ownership of capital is concentrated in the hands of elites.

THE GREAT RESET: A GLOBAL CABAL

In the West, after World War II and the rise of global social institutions, the world's wealthiest families, most prominent banks, and financial institutions have been pushing for a world government and international central bank they will control. This global cabal evolved into a plan for domination by elites who meet each year at the World Economic Forum (WEF) in Davos, Switzerland.

Klaus Schwab, Founder and Executive Chairman of the WEF, has made these goals public in his book *COVID-19: The Great Reset.*[5] The catchphrase, "own nothing and be happy,"[6] has been used to entice people to become a global serf in the society they want to control by 2030:

> Welcome to the year 2030. Welcome to my city—or should I say, "our city." I don't own anything. I don't own a car. I don't own a house. I don't own any appliances or any clothes.
>
> It might seem odd to you, but it makes perfect sense for us in this city. Everything you considered a product, has now become a service. We have access to transportation, accommodation, food and all the things we need in our daily lives. One by one all these things became free, so it ended up not making sense for us to own much.[7]

5. Klaus Schwab and Thierry Malleret, *COVID-19: The Great Reset* (Switzerland: ISBN Agentur Schweiz, July, 2020).
6. Ida Auken, "Welcome To 2030: I Own Nothing, Have No Privacy And Life Has Never Been Better," *Forbes,* November 10, 2016. https://www.forbes.com/sites/worldeconomicforum/2016/11/10/shopping-i-cant-really-remember-what-that-is-or-how-differently-well-live-in-2030/
    See also: https://m.facebook.com/watch/?v=10153920524981479&_rdr
7. Auken, Ibid.

The WEF describes a globalist utopia reminiscent of Edward Bellamy's novel *Looking Backward,* published in 1888:

> Julian West, a young Bostonian is put into a hypnotic sleep in the late nineteenth century and awakens in the year 2000 in a socialist utopia. Crime, war, personal animosity, and want are nonexistent. Equality of the sexes is a fact of life. In short, a messianic state of brotherly love is in effect.[8]

Ironically, the socialist utopia described in WEF propaganda is quite the opposite of what is being planned. Ordinary people may "own nothing," but they will not be happy. The WEF intends to install a world government and banking cabal exploiting the masses for the world's wealthiest elites. Th WEF will control all governments, people, and financial institutions. Any person that doesn't follow the plan will be given a low social credit score and instantly cut off from the electronic money they provide.

Klaus Schwab's utopia represents Karl Marx's greatest nightmare: the most extreme concentration of "bourgeois property" imaginable. The workers owning the means of production is out of the question. Already ordinary people are being asked to sacrifice while elites fly in corporate jets to sumptuous events for globalist planning. Justin Trudeau, Prime Minister of Canada and praised by Schwab as an exemplary disciple of the WEF, is investing Canadian resources in food made from insects rather than animal meat.[9] This is not a plan to make people happy.

THE BANK OF NORTH DAKOTA

Before discussing proposals for the distribution of new money to sovereign individuals, it is useful to discuss one public bank that supports

---

8. From the Amazon.com description of the 1996 Dover thrift edition of Edward Bellamy's *Looking Backward.* https://www.amazon.com/Looking-Backward-Dover-Thrift-Editions/dp/0486290387

9. Alessia Passafiume, "Why aren't we all eating insects yet?" *Toronto Star,* June 11, 2022. https://www.thestar.com/life/food_wine/2022/06/11/what-happened-to-the-edible-insect-food-revolution.html

community banks and the broader distribution of capital to citizens. The Bank of North Dakota (BND) was founded in 1919 to support the state's farmers. All of the state's revenues are deposited in the BND by law.

The BND acts like a mini-federal reserve. It serves as a clearing house for local banks and credit unions in its system. Accounts are not FDIC insured but guaranteed by the State of North Dakota. The advisory includes two members who are officers of banks whose stocks are majority owned by North Dakota residents. The BND does not provide retail services like ATMs but instead supports the capitalization of local banks and credit unions, giving them advantages over small banks in other states that enable them to compete with Wall Street Banks for loans:

> While locally owned small and mid-sized banks (under $10 billion in assets) account for only 30 percent of deposits nationally, in North Dakota they have 72 percent of the market.[10]

Returning money to the Treasury, the BND has a *distributive* effect, reducing the financial burden on all taxpayers. On the other hand, most central banks have a *concentrating* effect through debt-creation schemes. North Dakota does not print money and must maintain a balanced budget. The federal government is currently exempt from this fiscally responsible behavior.

The BND is involved in the same activities as other banks but has been conservative in its investments. The rules that govern the BND encourage decentralized community *personal* banking, which focuses on individual economic sovereignty. While the BND holds the mortgages and business loans originated by local banks, these mortgages are not bundled and sold on other secondary financial markets. While the BND has been a model for bank decentralization, it does not directly address the problem of the creation of new money through fractional reserve lending. However, since its profits are plowed back into the treasury, it reduces the debt burden on all taxpayers.

---

10. Ibid.

Universal Basic Income

> Universal basic income (UBI) is a government program in which every adult citizen receives a set amount of money regularly. The goals of a basic income system are to alleviate poverty and replace other need-based social programs that potentially require greater bureaucratic involvement.[11]

While never successfully implemented, UBI appeals when there is fear that machines will replace workers who will become unemployed. This was the argument by Andrew Yang in his 2020 presidential campaign. He proposed the government pay every American a $1,000 per month universal basic income. UBI does not change the ownership of capital, which would remain concentrated, but it would be more heavily taxed and redistributed as a form of welfare.

Yang's proposal is like the WEF "Great Reset" in that everyone will be taken care of by a benevolent elite in control of governments and the economy. There is no historical reason to believe such a system would work, quite the opposite.

In the United States, the robotics and AI industries have changed the nature of human labor, but they have not produced massive unemployment in a free and competitive market. The cost to fund Yang's proposal would be $2.8 trillion annually. Alaska and Norway have the only successful programs that distribute money to citizens. These programs are supported by oil revenue profits that produce a government surplus, not based on debt. These programs distribute funds from natural resources considered the property of all citizens. This is similar to Ken Wilber's idea of an integral commons.[12] Alaska's program is universal but not basic income. It only pays $1,000 to $2,000 per year per person. Norway pays for college education and other welfare benefits, but this is not a UBI.

COVID-19 basic income checks revealed the flaw in Yang's UBI theory. This distribution was paid for by printing fiat money from

---

11. Katelyn Peters, "Universal Basic Income (UBI)," *Investopedia,* https://www.investopedia.com/terms/b/basic-income.asp

12. See Figure 6, Appendix. This is stage 8 in the lower right quadrant.

government debt. The result proved disastrous. Since the debt did not lead to production, but created more money and less production, it caused inflation that more than offset the original value of the distributions. The sixteen percent inflation caused a person earning $50,000 to lose $8,000 in purchasing power, more than twice the stimulus checks that were issued. UBI is a quick prescription for economic collapse. The Social Security Trust Fund, on the other hand, has worked because distributions come from savings created by insurance premiums collected by employers. It is based on savings, not debt.

UBI does not redistribute capital ownership of the means of production, helping people to become economically sovereign. Instead, it tends to cause economic dependency on the government, reduces sovereignty, and causes economic collapse.

BINARY ECONOMICS, ESOPS, AND CSOPS

> Binary Economics offers a conception of economics that is foundationally distinct from the economic theories presently employed by government, private enterprise, charitable institutions, and individuals to formulate and evaluate economic policy.[13]

Binary economics explains income from two sources: capital and labor. Louis Kelso, the originator of binary economics, explained:

> (1) labor and capital are equally fundamental or "binary" factors of production, (2) technology makes capital much more productive than labor, (3) the more broadly capital is acquired with the earnings of capital the faster the economy will grow.[14]

Kelso stated that labor accounted for 95 percent of the production of goods when the U.S. was founded. Wealthy aristocrats, 5 percent of the population, controlled most of the capital. But labor, not capital, was the basis of production. Ownership of property was widely distributed.

---

13. Ashford, Robert, "Binary Economics: An Overview" (2010). Syracuse University College of Law - Faculty Scholarship. 15. https://surface.syr.edu/lawpub/15

14. Ibid.

Each person owned one unit of labor production. That produced relative economic equality. This could be called economic democracy.

Early U.S. society was different from the capitalist societies in Europe that Karl Marx criticized. Marx was concerned with the ownership of private property by "capitalists." Kelso argued that inequality does not come from the of ownership of "private property" but its concentration. Marxists made the mistake of thinking in unitary economics: that all production value is based on labor. A statement from the communist party shows this mistaken view:

> Abolition of private property means stripping billionaire investors of the ability to get rich from our labor.[15]

Kelso said the binary economic situation had reversed as the United States approached the year 2000. Capital accounted for over 90 percent of production.[16] The owners of capital no longer needed as much labor to produce basic goods. They were earning a profit from production by machines. This has caused some people to argue human beings, as laborers, are expendable and there is a surplus population in the world. These views exist among leaders of the World Economic Forum (WEF):

> Yuval Noah Harari, historian, futurist, and World Economic Forum adviser, said, "We just don't need the vast majority of the population" in the early 21st century given modern technologies' rendering human labor economically and militarily "redundant."[17]

Harari reveals an elitist view by saying, "we don't need." Who is the "we" that doesn't need other human beings? Members of the WEF? Human beings have intrinsic value, and their labor value is not their only value. Seeing humans only for labor value violates Kant's Categorical

---

15. Scott Hiley, "Abolition of Private Property?" Communist Party USA, January 4, 2018. https://www.cpusa.org/interact_cpusa/the-father-of/ Italics mine.

16. Louis O. Kelso interview by Harold Channer. https://www.youtube.com/watch?v=lRPT3SFkndA.

17. Robert Kraychik. "WEF Adviser Yuval Harari: 'We Just Don't Need the Vast Majority of the Population' in Today's World, *Breibart,* August 10, 2022.

Imperative never to treat others as merely a means but as ends in themselves.[18] The Christian argument that every person is a child of God implies this categorical imperative. In Ken Wilber's *Theory of Everything,* seeing others as having intrinsic value comes with developing a second-tier consciousness.[19] A second-tier consciousness is necessary for an integral society.

Harari presents an image of a very dystopian future "where artificial intelligence 'knows us better than we know ourselves'; and where godlike elites and super-intelligent robots consider the rest of humanity to be superfluous."[20] He refers to people as "economically useless."[21]

Harari's future is a nightmare based on the current form of capitalism in which elites and financial industries receive the fruits of fractional reserve banking in economic feudalism. However, the future proposed in this book is one of "economic democracy." It sees the WEF's understanding of banking and capitalism as corrupt and unjust in which elites steal the "new money" from the masses.

All human beings have an equal right to their labor and income from capital. One class should not profit from the capital, while another class is limited to income from labor, becoming superfluous. An integral society should primarily be one middle class that derives income from capital and labor. Kelso argues that the current welfare system in the United States is based on redistribution, and it has reached its limitation as more production is created by capital and less by labor.[22]

Following Kelso, most binary economists today seek ways to avoid the problems of welfare for "surplus labor" by enabling the working class to earn income from capital. There are several voluntary market-based

18. Immanuel Kant, *Groundwork of the Metaphysic of Morals* (San Francisco: Harper Torchbooks, 1956), pp. 96-97.

19. Ken Wilber, *A Theory of Everything*, pp. 12-13.

20. Bill Gates, "What if people run out of things to do?" GatesNotes, May 22, 2017.

21. Yuval Noah Harari interview, World Thought Leaders, https://www.youtube.com/watch?v=biKwkMJHlOM

22. Louis O. Kelso interview by Harold Channer. https://www.youtube.com/watch?v=lRPT3SFkndA.

strategies proposed for distributing capital without a social revolution and theft. Mechanisms should exist to enable people not born with capital to acquire it.

Economic inequality will not be solved by owners of capital providing jobs or money to the poor and unemployed people. That is serfdom and economic feudalism. It is based on the unitary view that treats the masses as laborers only. Mechanisms for the distribution of the ownership of machines and AI used for the production of the majority of goods are needed for economic democracy.

Kelso promoted Employee Stock Option Plans (ESOPs) as one solution. Workers would become shareholders and own a part of the means of production, sharing profits from stock dividends in the companies for which they worked.

For ESOPs to work well, corporations need to pay dividends so that profits are divided among the employee-owners. The tax structure needs to be changed for this to happen. Currently, corporations are taxed on profits before dividends. This motivates them not to issue dividends, but to spend profits on their executive bonuses and luxuries. Ethical laws would not tax profits before dividends are paid. That violates individual economic sovereignty and an act of government theft from its citizens. Instead, the government should require the payment of dividends to the individual shareholders. The shareholders, in turn, would pay an income tax to the government on their dividends and other income. This way, the government acts as a referee, treating individuals, not corporations or itself, as sovereign. With such laws, more production would be encouraged, profits widely distributed to workers, and the unjust double taxation of dividends would be fixed.

Consumer Stock Ownership Plans (CSOPs) are a method to distribute company stock to those who buy products or use public utilities like subways. A variation on cash-back bonuses that comes with credit card services, CSOPs would give shares of company stock on a percentage of the purchases.

ESOPs and CSOPs would gradually distribute the ownership of

capital throughout society, and owners of these share would earn an income from both capital and their own labor. Other stock distribution proposals include MUSOPs (Mutual Stock Ownership Plans), GSOPs (General Stock Ownership Plans), ICOPs (Individual Capital Ownership plans), COMCOPs (Commercial Capital Ownership Plans), PUBCOPs (Public Capital Ownership Plans) and RECOPs (Residential Capital Ownership Plans).[23] All these stock distribution proposals would distribute some ownership of productive capital. Still, these forms of stock distribution do not address the more significant problem of growing economic disparity caused by the concentration of new money through fractional reserve banking. One proposal to address this problem is to distribute new money directly to all people through Capital Homestead Accounts.

CAPITAL HOMESTEAD ACCOUNTS

Capital Homestead Accounts (CHAs) are an industrial-age version of land homesteads given to settlers of "new land" after the Civil War.[24] This act provided 160 acres of land for a filing fee, allowing everyone to become economically independent, distributing a common resource, land, offering recipients economic sovereignty. Norway uses a common resource, oil revenue, to fund college educations, assisting students in gaining economic sovereignty. This is an investment in human capital required for labor in capital-intensive economies.

New money can be viewed as a common resource distributed to provide economic sovereignty. In the discussion of fractional reserve banking, it was shown that large sums of new money get created, fueling economic expansion. Who gets this new money? Bank? The Government Treasury? Bank depositors? Or is it a resource to be shared by everyone?

Dr. Norman Kurland of the Center for Economic and Social Justice

23. Louis O. Kelso, *Democracy and Economic Power: Extending the ESOP Revolution through Binary Economics,* Part II,

24. Passed on May 20, 1862, the Homestead Act accelerated the settlement of the western territory by granting adult heads of families 160 acres of surveyed public land for a minimal filing fee and five years of continuous residence on that land. *National Archives.* https://www.archives.gov/milestone-documents/homestead-act.

(CESJ) believes the latter. He has proposed Capital Homestead Accounts to distribute new money to every citizen, creating a just and democratic economy.[25] Kurland describes this as a third way, neither an elite cabal nor communist seizure of capital. Instead, it is a distribution of common resources in the form of new money to use for production.

Kurland's "third way" would treat new money creation as a common resource. CHAs would functionally replace individual savings accounts, because those account would no longer earn an income. Rather, each citizen would receive a portion of the "new money" as a capital credit managed by a government agency. Banks would not receive the principal loan payments, but only a service fee. The loan payments would go to a government agency and distributed equally to all CHAs This would distributing the new money as equitably and widely as possible.

Kurland has suggested that based on average economic growth, CHAs could produce enough income to guarantee a basic retirement income and eventually replace Social Security. For example, the U.S. economy grew by $4 trillion in 2019, providing each CHA with a credit of $10,000. After 65 years, at this rate, this would amount to $650,000.

CHAs would be a positive alternative to Universal Basic Income (UBI) because they would create economic independence instead of dependency. Recipients would be sovereigns instead of serfs. CHAs would fulfill the ideals of communism by distributing the ownership of the means of production while avoiding the failure of communism caused by the control of the capital by a political party.

CHA's could serve at least five significant economic functions:

1. Motivate everyone to invest in economic, stimulating economic growth.

2. Assist people in attaining personal economic sovereignty through both labor and capital income.

3. Establish a personal pension fund for retirement, eliminating the

---

25. "Capital Homestead Accounts (CHAs)," The Center for Economic and Social Justice https://www.cesj.org/economic-democracy-vehicles/capital-homestead-accounts-chas/

need for Social Security and shrinking government entitlements.

4. As capital production replaces labor production, all people would have the opportunity to obtain capital, eliminating the problem of surplus labor.

5. Reduce the government ability to unethically create and spend new money by eliminating the current government/ bankcabals.

The Center for Economic and Social Justice (CESJ) has proposed an Economic Democracy Act (EDA) that could operate by modifying the current U.S. banking system that keeps but alters the mission of the Federal Reserve.[26] This includes deposits to CHAs and restructuring taxes to encourage capital production and distribution. The CESJ approach relies on the traditional lending approach to creating new money. Instead, new money being created by fractional reserve banking would be calculated from the growth of the economy and distributed as capital credit.

Conclusion

A republic based on the sovereign rights of individuals requires personal economic sovereignty to pursue happiness. This sovereignty existed as labor income when the United States was founded. However, the amount of labor required for producing goods and services was displaced by the industrial machines that require large amounts of capital. Through unethical practices that concentrated new capital in one to three percent of the population, economic feudalism and serfdom were created. Everyone should benefit from a societies economic growth, not just a few overlords.

New capital can be distributed widely among the citizens in several ways, including principal payments on bank loans given to depositors, or being divided among everyone in CHAs. Tax laws that did not tax corporate profits before stock dividends were dispersed would enable widespread ownership of corporate stocks. All citizens can have an equal

---

26. "How the Economic Democracy Act Would Change the System," Center for Economic and Social Justice. https://www.cesj.org/learn/economic-democracy-act/

opportunity to fund the corporations that generate wealth.

Since CHAs are unproven and involve a third party to manage distribution, I would recommend beginning with the proven method of lending from savings accounts in which principal payments, the new money, is paid to depositors while the bank charges interest for its service. However, CHAs seem to also be an ethical approach if the system is approved by the consent of the governed in a genuine system of representative government (not captured by political parties).

Of course the just distribution of capital would negatively impact those who feed off the corrupt system. Banks would only earn "labor income" through service fees, while capital income would be dispersed among the people, creating economic democracy. Also, governments would not have a secret way of getting new money, but they would have to go directly to the citizens to get funds for spending. This would return the House of Representatives to its primary mission of overseeing the expenditure of the taxpayers' money.

An integral economic system is one where everyone owns the fruits of there labor and capital ownership is widely distributed throughout society, enabling all people to become economic sovereigns. This should occur through an evolutionary and nonviolent approach that redirects unethical new money flows without depriving anyone of their current property. The banking business would not end, but it would be limited to honestly serving depositors and borrowers. Governments would no longer have access to new money. Government notes, instead of being held by a central bank, would need to be purchased from citizens.

Chapter 13

Social Institutions in a Constitutional Framework

The Declaration of an Integral Society and a Constitution of an Integral Society began the first two chapters of this book. This was followed with a history of the evolution of integral society is grounded upon the concept of personal sovereignty. We argued that the three spontaneous orders of human society are a part of human nature and that social institutions have evolved in three spheres as human beings seek advanced ways to communicate, learn, produce, exchange, and govern.

In the brief historical presentation, it is shown how some earlier societies prospered individual experienced autonomy or personal sovereignty where able to pursue happiness. We noted significant social evolution milestones in Babylon and the Roman Republic, where there was a large middle class, widespread upward mobility, and ownership of property.

The ancient world collapsed with the centralization of social institutions, church and state, that caused and supported feudalism. Ownership of the property was concentrated in the hands of feudal lords. The Church and the Emperors controlled knowledge, land, and power. Individual sovereignty reemerged over several hundred years. People secured religious and political freedoms and economic sovereignty that enabled the rise of modern liberal democracies. These democracies had a republican form of government that had checks and balances on power and guaranteed individual rights, equality under the law, and due process.

Individual sovereignty was the focus of the U.S. Declaration of Independence, and the U.S. Constitution became widespread in Western legal thought. The American Revolution abolished the two largest corporations of the time, the East India Company and the Hudson's Bay Company. Most Americans were self-employed on family farms and businesses, giving them economic sovereignty. If historian Edward Gibbon were alive today, he might argue that best time and place to live would be in the United States in the second half of the 20th century.

However, like Ancient Rome, that period in the United States was fraught with underlying problems of social institutions that would deprive individuals of their sovereignty, consolidate control, and devise new forms of feudalism. Since the 18th century, industrial corporations, financial institutions, banks, governments, universities, and the mass media have been morphing into social institutions that use, abuse, and exploit people instead of staying true to their missions to serve people. and many other types of social institutions have arisen and gradually taken that sovereignty away from individual citizens. Political parties have taken sovereignty away from individuals in the sphere of governance, the mass media in the sphere of culture, and financial firms in the economic sphere. The Constitution of the United States ,, created in the 18th century, did not address the future development of these social institutions.

The system was designed so that vigilant citizens could create laws that would curtail abuses and corruption of the social system. But citizens were not vigilant, as long as their autonomy was not too restricted, they accepted the leadership and behavior of the social institutions that were created. There were some successes. Civil rights legislation brought legal equality for minorities and women. The Glass-Steagall Act prevented banks from speculating with depositors' money.

Most changes have benefited social institutions at the expense of citizens. The 16th and 17 Amendments removed essential checks and balances. Supreme Court rulings related to "corporate personhood"[1] gave

---

1. John Witt interview, "What Is The Basis For Corporate Personhood?" *NPRnews,* October 24, 2011. https://www.npr.org/2011/10/24/141663195/what-is-the-basis-for-corporate-personhood.

moneyed interests influence over politicians. Federal law enforcement and intelligence agencies were weaponized against citizens who criticized official policy, depriving them of self-rule. The sovereignty of institutions has become equal to or greater than the sovereignty of individual people.

Current Western governance systems have been referred to as plutocracy, oligarchy, partyocracy, fascism, an administrative state, tyranny, and combinations thereof. It is governance by and for social institutions at the expense of the citizens who have been significantly displaced from the legislative process. Most social institutions have a legitimate place in society when they serve their original mission in helping sovereign individuals in some way. When social institutions are abused and hijacked by unscrupulous leaders or financial and ideological interests, they violate individual sovereignty and become a drain on society rather than a contribution.

A constitution for an integral society needs to be a framework for a society of sovereign citizens in the post-modern world with its complex social institutions in all three spheres. Chapters 9-12 discussed significant problems related to legislation, ethics, and distribution of wealth that a constitution and new laws need to address.

The remainder of this chapter discuss a few additional problems addressed in the Declaration and proposed articles of a Constitution of an Integral Society in the opening chapters. Key points to keep in mind for a Constitution are:

1. Individuals are sovereign; institutions serve them.

2. Life, liberty, property, and the pursuit of happiness are components of individual sovereignty.

3. Social institutions must be kept to their mission.

4. Social institutions should be at the lowest possible level of society.

5. Social institutions should be kept in their appropriate sphere.

6. Conflicts of interest should be avoided.

7. The citizens are the owners of public commons.

The following sections sum up problems discussed and raise some additional problems in contemporary society that are addressed in the prosed articles of a Constitution of an Integral Society.

DISESTABLISHMENT OF POLITICAL PARTIES AND OTHER IDENTITY GROUPS

The disestablishment of religion was the first step in limiting a social institution to its sphere. This principle should apply to all groups and social institutions. The freedom of religion, speech, press, and assembly is necessary for individual sovereignty. This is enshrined in the First Amendment to the Constitution:

> Congress shall make no law respecting an establishment of religion, or prohibiting the free exercise thereof; or abridging the freedom of speech, or of the press; or the right of the people peaceably to assemble, and to petition the Government for a redress of grievances.

The establishment clause, "there shall be no law respecting an establishment of religion," is necessary for the free exercise of religion. No official religion can be forced upon people through the power of government, nor should the government subsidize a religion. The same principle applies to the establishment of a press, which could be used to force one version of the truth on the people as was the case with *Pravda* (truth) in the USSR. There the government controlled information through one newspaper and radio station.

Less discussed is the establishment of any other group, the counterpart to freedom of assembly. Establishing any group means making the purpose of the group the a goal of the government. This is a restriction on the freedom of sovereign individuals. The most severe oversight in the first amendment is political parties, which should be free to assemble but not to control legislation. When a law or legislative rule supports or "establishes" political parties, or any cultural or financial institution, that social institution, which has more resources than an individual, takes the reigns of government from the citizens.

At the U.S. founding, cultural identity was primarily religious. People identified with other groups, largely community based, but they were local and not a threat political, religious, or economic freedom. After eight years of experience with the new government, it was clear to the founders that the Constitution had not adequately limited political parties. In his farewell address, George Washington wrote at length about the dangers of party:

> The alternate domination of one faction over another, sharpened by the spirit of revenge natural to party dissension, which in different ages and countries has perpetrated the most horrid enormities, is itself a frightful despotism. But this leads at length to a more formal and permanent despotism. The disorders and miseries which result gradually incline the minds of men to seek security and repose in the absolute power of an individual, and sooner or later the chief of some prevailing faction, more able or more fortunate than his competitors, turns this disposition to the purposes of his own elevation on the ruins of public liberty.
>
> Without looking forward to an extremity of this kind (which nevertheless ought not to be entirely out of sight), the common and continual mischiefs of the spirit of party are sufficient to make it the interest and duty of a wise people to discourage and restrain it.
>
> It serves always to distract the public councils and enfeeble the public administration. It agitates the community with ill-founded jealousies and false alarms; kindles the animosity of one part against another; foments occasionally riot and insurrection. It opens the door to foreign influence and corruption, which find a facilitated access to the government itself through the channels of party passion. Thus the policy and the will of one country are subjected to the policy and will of another.[2]

The failure to heed Washington's warning has given us the tribal rivalries between political parties today. Two parties have established

---

2. George Washington, "Farewell Address," *American Daily Advertiser* (Philadelphia), September 19, 1796. https://www.presidency.ucsb.edu/documents/farewell-address.

themselves in the government. The clearest example of establishment is having their names on ballots. The Constitution stated that the members of the House of Representatives would be chosen by the people,[3] not by political parties. Party names on ballots prejudices the voter with a party bias, establishing this bias in the governance process.

Imagine if after the names of candidates on ballots were followed by Christian, Muslim, Jew, or Atheist instead of Republican, Democrat, Libertarian, or Communist, the spirit of faction would be equally destructive. The First Amendment restrains a religion from being on the ballot but not a party. This needs to be corrected. Associating individuals with groups on ballots allows those groups to hijack the election process and violate individual sovereignty.

Placing the party name after a candidate on a ballot is also a mechanism of party control over the candidate. Parties endorse candidates who promise to work for the party platform and vote in lockstep with the party chair. They will vote for the special interests that lobby the party for government favors instead of the interests of sovereign citizens. Political parties have become the primary vehicle for special interests to hijack the legislative process and corrupt politicians. This voting process enables parties to hijack representative democracy.

Political parties have found many ways to act as legislative vehicles special interests and circumvent the goal of "the consent of the governed."[4] Omnibus bills that contain more than one subject are the most obvious way special "pork" gets stuffed into a bill. This violates the concept of single subject legislation in which voters can hold legislators accountable for how they voted on each item. These party-driven processes need to be removed. Line item vetoes and term limits can help eliminate entrenched corruption, but disestablishing political parties and other identity groups is the most critical fix.

---

3.   U.S. Constitution, Article 1, Section 2: "The House of Representatives shall be composed of Members chosen every second Year by the People of the several States..."

4.   The Declaration of Independence declared "—That to secure these rights, Governments are instituted among Men, deriving their just powers from the consent of the governed,"

In conclusion, the First Amendment should be revised to say "Congress shall make no law respecting an establishment of any religion, political party, or other group, or prohibiting the free exercise thereof."

REPEAL THE 16TH AND 17TH AMENDMENTS

The 16th and 17th Amendments to the Constitution were acts that took power away from sovereign individuals and the states. These Amendments were necessary to establish the Federal Reserve and a government/banking cabal. They directly opposed and partly dismantled the original Constitution.

The 16th Amendment gave the Federal government the power to directly tax the citizens' incomes "without apportionment among the several States, and without regard to any census or enumeration."[5] The Constitution was designed for a federation of states that each had their own rules on taxing citizens. The 16th Amendment was necessary for the Federal Reserve Act,[6] making individual citizens responsible for the government debt that the new cabal would create.

The Constitution originally allowed only the states to tax citizens directly. The Founders were still aware of the Stamp Act,[7] a direct tax levied on colonists by Parliament. That tax led to the cry "no taxation without representation" and eventually the Revolutionary War. Colonists believed they should only pay direct taxes to their representative assemblies in their colonies that became states.

Like the Stamp Act, the 16th Amendment skipped a level of governance and directly laid a tax on citizens. This violates the principle of economic subsidiarity, which is a principle of an integral society.

---

5. Passed by Congress on July 2, 1909, and ratified February 3, 1913, the 16th amendment established Congress's right to impose a Federal income tax.

6. On December 23, 1913, the Senate adopted the conference report by a vote of 43 to 25, with every Democrat present voting for the measure and all but four Republicans voting against it. (Twenty-seven senators were "paired" or chose not to vote.) Most senators immediately rushed to Union Station to catch trains home for the holidays,

7. Parliament passed the Stamp Act on March 22, 1765 and repealed it in 1766, but issued a Declaratory Act reaffirming its authority to pass any colonial legislation.

The 17th Amendment stated that Senators would be "elected by the people of each State."[8] The Constitution was originally stated that each state legislature would appoint two Senators. The 17th Amendment eliminated the states' ability to block federal legislation that exploited their citizens. The Senate had been a layer of protection for sovereign individuals. This Amendment removed the direct representation of states in their own union. This violated the principle of subsidiarity and removed an essential check and balance on legislative power. In Chapter 8, "Elites and the People: Legislation in an Integral Society," this problem is discussed at length.

FORBID BANKS FROM THEFT OF PROFIT ON DEPOSITS

Taken together, the 16th and 17th Amendments and the Federal Reserve Act enabled the creation of the corrupt federal bank cabal that thrives on a process of theft from citizens through an unethical form of fractional reserve banking. This common banking practice is the most serious cause of economic injustice in the world. Chapter 11 explains this process in detail.

The purpose of banks is to store, lend, and manage money for customers, not to invest or speculate with their money. The history of banking shows that honest banking works when banks receive fees for their services. This fee provides bank employees and owners with labor income.

Fractional reserve banking can be safely used to create new money with adequate reserves and loan insurance. Banks and governments are not the rightful owners of new money. Ways to distribute new money are discussed in Chapters 11 and 12.

REQUIRE UNTAXED CORPORATE DIVIDENDS

Governments deprive shareholders of profits by directly taxing corporate profits before dividends are distributed to owners. Then, if dividends

---

8. The 17th Amendment of the U.S. Constitution, passed May 13, 1912 and ratified April 8, 1913.

are paid, the shareholder pay tax on them as personal income. With this double tax, governments deprive citizens the fruits of ownership of the means of production and steal from citizens. There are other bad consequences that result: (1) corporations are motivated to give large payments to employees as bonuses instead of the government and forget dividends; (2) corporations are motivated to break even and not reinvest profit in economic expansion that gets taxed as increased net worth; and, (3) corporation/government cabals develop in which corporate profits get divided between the government and high-paid executives.

These problems can be remedied by laws that forbid the government from taking any corporate tax before dividends are distributed and requiring the distribution of profits to shareholders. The dividend income received by shareholders should then be taxed as personal income at the same rate as their wage income. This would lead to wide and more just distribution of capital income. Government would get its rightful share from the owners of the company through personal income tax, rather than acting as a corporate raider causing corporations to pay top executives exorbitant salaries.

Forbid Stock Broker Control of Corporations

Another issue related to the true ownership of capital relates to capital management by investment brokers and funds. The public became aware of representatives of mutual funds sitting on corporate boards when Elon Musk offered to buy Twitter. It was announced that Vanguard owned 82.4 million shares. Does Vanguard really own these shares or are they using investments of their investors who are the true owners?

We have discussed that banks are not the true owners of the savings deposits, and the depositors should paid the principal on loans from their savings. Similarly, stock brokers and mutual funds are not the owners of share, but the investors. On their website, Vanguard proudly proclaims this:

Vanguard isn't owned by shareholders. It's owned by the people who invest in our funds.[9]

When a representative of Vanguard sat on Twitter's board, he represented the entire Vanguard's portfolio, not the shareholder's interest in Twitter. What is best for Twitter might not be what is best for Vanguard as a group. There is a built in conflict of interest. Vanguard might be interested in sacrificing one company in its portfolio to give a monopoly to another. Or it might want to own shares in all producers of a product to create a cartel. Allowing a broker to make decisions for corporations and shareholders is like allowing banks to speculate with depositor's money.

In *Woke Inc.*, Vivek Ramaswamy discussed the nature of this problem. He described how this new layer of "ownership" does not function as the traditional relationship between "owners and managers." Vanguard placing a representative on the board of Twitter creates a conflict between "owners and owners."[10] Or, more accurately a conflict between real owners and financial institutions acting as owners.

As a broker, an investment service should receive a fee for its servicer, but should be forbidden to tamper with corporation decisions. Its mission should be restricted to acting as a broker for investors who are the true owners of the companies. Laws like the Glass-Steagall Act, which limits banks to banking, should exist to limit brokers to brokering. There are significant conflicts of interest between the owners of an investment firm and the true owners of the shares and the corporation.

APPOINTMENTS OF COURT JUSTICES

Political appointments, especially partisan appointments, can be highly divisive and weaponized against members of another political party. Appointments can be used to embed a party, or another group, in key positions, hijacking the state apparatus. If the President or other person appointing a judge or official is firmly committed to a political party or

---

9. Vanguard Corporate Portal. https://investor.vanguard.com/corporate-portal/

10. Vivek Ramaswamy, *Woke, Inc.: Inside Corporate America's Social Justice Scam* (New York: Center Street-Hachette), 2021.

religious group, for example the Muslim Brotherhood, he can appoint people who do not believe in equal treatment under the law.

The best process possible should be employed to ensure that judges and administrators are highly qualified for their job and impartial in their decisions. Too often, political leaders appoint people based on their loyalty to some group or ideology, not on their skill or commitment to the Constitution and the sovereignty of citizens. Such appointments can also be "sold" in "pay-for-play" corruption schemes. Better methods of appointment are often required to ensure judges and government officials serve individual citizens and not special interest groups.

The way to think about this problem is to ask, what to we want of the judge or administrator? The main answers are knowledge of the job, skill, experience, and impartial service to sovereign citizens. Then we ask about best ways to achieve this. The process should be like a job interview on behalf of the citizens. Civil service exam results and prior performance are necessary, but how do you prevent control of the official by financial or partisan interests? One method to prevent any interest group from controlling the appointment is selection by lottery from among several qualified candidates.

In the case of the Supreme Court justices, we have seen general support for greater federal power because appointments are made by federal officials. However, the Supreme Court, should serve individuals and the states. One possibility for appointing justices that were both politically neutral and respected the principle of subsidiarity would be to have states nominate qualified judges and then select them by lottery. While individual candidates will still have personal biases, the overall makeup of the Court would be more representative of the country.

Department heads usually need prior experience and often are promoted through the ranks. Lotteries may not be as applicable, but efforts to focus on skill and avoid partisanship are important. Approval by the Senate seems appropriate (1) if parties are not embedded in the government by an impartial voting process and (2) the Senate is composed of seasoned states-persons appoint by the states. Those two fixes are discussed earlier.

SALARIES OF MEMBERS OF CONGRESS AND STAFF

It is a conflict of interest for Congress or any agency of the federal government to set and pay the salaries of members of Congress. Representatives, like other people, will work for those who pay their wages. Members of Congress and their staff will serve the interests of their constituents better, when the states pay their salary. But it is appropriate for the Federal government to provide their office space. States paying the costs of their representatives and staff is an appropriate state responsibility derived from the principle of subsidiarity. It is also a check against their misuse of the federal budget for personal gain.

FORBID ARMING FEDERAL AGENTS

The intent of the Second Amendment to the U.S. Constitution is to prevent federal standing armies, or armed federal agents from having the power to suppress citizens by force of arms. Except for Federal military services used outside its borders or for the protection of the President, who is the Commander in Chief, or military bases in the Federation, no arms should be issued by the Federation to its agents or employees.

Government employees should have the same right to purchase arms as private citizens for personal protection. This is an essential protection against Federal tyranny and top-down power flow.

CONCLUSION
The recommendations in this chapter address legal changes to limit conflicts of interest, schemes for theft, and the concentrations and abuses of power of social institutions. This chapter has highlighted several significant problems not addressed in the U.S. Constitution and several other problems where the original intent of the Constitution has been circumvented by constitutional amendments or corrupt legislative and financial practices that are legal but unethical. The proposed articles of a Constitution for an Integral in Chapter 2 address these issues.

Epilogue

The evolutionary development of integral society and the constitution for an integral society discussed in this book are meant to convey a vision of what in integral society is and some of the mechanisms that can be employed to achieve it. As societies worldwide work to improve the ability of sovereign citizens to pursue happiness, they can adapt by applying principles of a higher social consciousness than experienced in a world of dictators, oligarchs, military elites, bank cabals, and the unchecked behavior of social institutions.

Social institutions exist at many levels and in three primary spheres. Our analysis focused primarily on the level of a federation of states. This level in earlier times was the level of empire, where many kingdoms were under an emperor. We focused on this level of governance because of the impact of dysfunctional federal-level social systems on the world today, and their proclivity for oppression, corruption, war, and exploitation. This applies to the United States, the United Kingdom, the European Union, the Russian Federation, China, and India. These societies have a common military security zone and a single currency. We could also envision a greater federation of the Middle Eastern states, African states, and South American states.

The Constitution of a Republican society that protects the sovereignty of its citizens is a social operating system. Computer programmers devise different operating systems o produce similar ends. Apple's IOS, Microsoft's Windows, and the Android operating systems all serve similar computer functionality. A state-level and federal-level operating system will have differences, because the social institutions (the hardware) they connect will be different.

The Constitution for an Integral Society presented in the last chapter is developed on the U.S. Constitution to address the social problems discussed in the previous chapters. In the United States, it may not be necessary to replace the current operating system with an entirely new system but develop an "upgrade" that includes a lot of anti-virus protection against institutional corruption and abuse. Something similar was done after the Civil War with the Constitution's 13th, 14th, and 15th amendments. That was an "upgrade" to address the problems of slavery. Today in the U.S. there is a different type of civil war between the average citizens and elites controlling social institutions. An upgrade could be applied that (1) repeals the 16th and 17th amendments, (2) adds amendments about money and banking, and (3) expands the First Amendment from the separation of church and state to the separation of all social organizations from the state.

It is, of course, possible that legislatures could pass individual laws instead of changing the constitution. However, the analysis of human nature and institutional nature discussed, particularly related to political parties and the abuse of public money, makes this unlikely to happen. We saw that the Glass-Steagall Act, excellent legislation, was repealed under pressure from the financial industries. Further, the political parties that have hijacked the legislative process will not promote legislation that reduces their activity to their proper role and voluntarily return power to the citizens.

The evolutionary path for other federal-level governance structures will be different. In some cases, the dictatorial power of a president must be reduced, in others embedded political parties or religions must step aside, and some regions need more organization to improve security and trade. This integral vision will provide different evolutionary paths for societies toward functional and efficient regional governance that serves individual sovereignty in a complex world of social institutions.

The evolutionary path requires that a more highly developed cultural consciousness precedes the implementation of constitutional changes in a society. This is necessary to have genuine consent of the governed and not masses of people cajoled by pandering politicians claiming to know what is best for the people. The informed consent of the governed is the only legitimate basis for a social contract between sovereign individuals and governance institutions.

Appendix

An Integral Framework: Brief Overview with Diagrams

INTEGRAL CONSCIOUSNESS

Integral theory is based on the development of human consciousness. Consciousness develops in individuals from egocentric to transpersonal and beyond as they learn from others, life experiences, and seek higher levels of consciousness. Integral society requires enough individuals attaining integral consciousness to raise cultural consciousness and social institutions to an integral level.

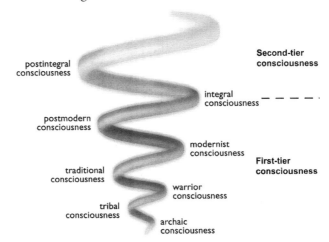

Figure 4. The Spiral of Development in Consciousness and Culture
© Steve McIntosh, *Integral Consciousness and the Future of Evolution,* Paragon House, 2007, p. 34. Reprinted with permission.

Ken Wilber divides consciousness into two tiers. First-tier consciousness is inadequately developed to sustain an integral society. Second-tier consciousness is required for a functional integral society in which social institutions serve individual sovereignty.

QUADRANTS AND SPHERES

In *A Theory of Everything*,[1] Wilber places all of society into four quadrants. They are related to the interior and exterior aspects of individuals and society.

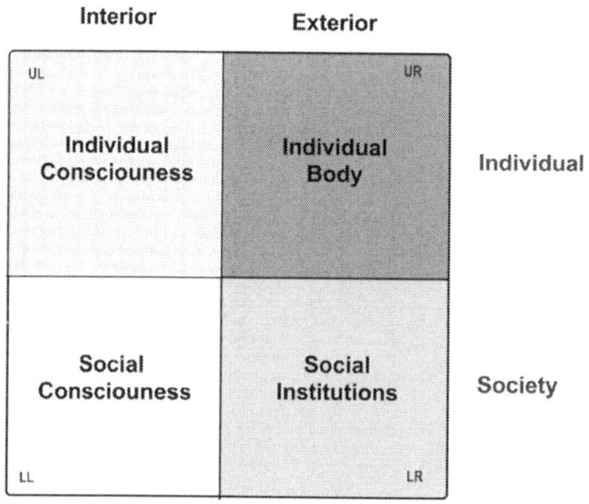

Figure 5. Four Quadrants of Human Life

The upper two quadrants refer to the individual. The upper left (UL) is consciousness, and the upper right (UR) the body and external activities. The lower quadrants refer to society. The lower left (LL) is social consciousness, and the lower right (LR) social institutions and other external aspects of society.

Human beings have always lived with these four quadrants. The nature and complexity of the quadrants evolves in levels and spheres as civilizations develops, Social evolution is associated with advances in all four quadrants, radiating from the center outward.

1. Ken Wilber, *A Theory of Everything: An Integral Vision for Business, Politics, Science, and Spirituality* (Boston: Shambhala, 2001).

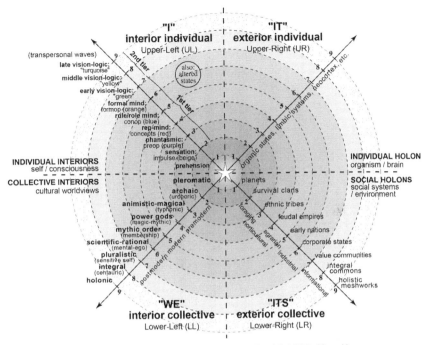

Reprinted from Brad Reynolds, *Where's Wilber At*, p. 178, © Copyright 2006 Brad Reynolds.

Figure 6. Evolution of Society in Four Quadrants. Each ring is a "holon."

In Figure 6, the lower right quadrant shows the evolution of external society. This book discusses social evolution from stages 2 to 8, from survival clans to integral commons. We focus on the rise of social institutions, their early anarchic and abusive nature, and their transformation into a functional integral society.

Wilber calls each circle on this diagram a "holon." At each stage or level of external development, there are corresponding developments in all other quadrants. Consciousness and knowledge must expand at each level to support society's increased complexity. As social consciousness increases, higher levels of social organization are possible, from families to tribes, cities, states, regional, and global organization. Institutions at each level and in each sphere of society have unique purposes and functions in an integral society.

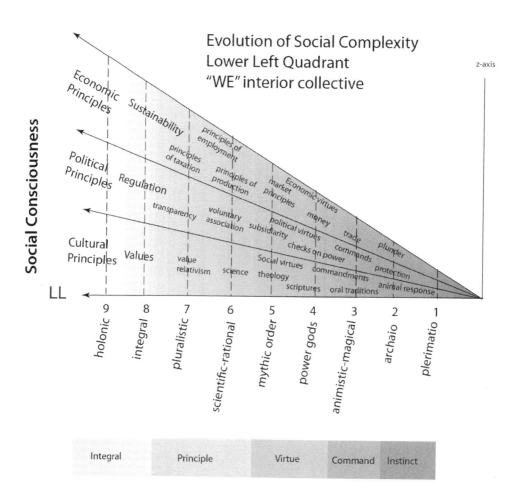

Figure 7. The Internal Evolution of Social Institutions in Three Spheres, Lower Left Quadrant, z-axis. © Gordon L. Anderson

The complexity of social consciousness and social institutions can be illustrated on the z-axis rising up from the lower two quadrants. The evolution of social institutions and spheres is shown in Figures 7 and 8. Stages 1-9 refer to Figure 6. Figure 4 refers to social consciousness, and Figure 5 to the corresponding institutions. Wilber did not discuss the z-axis; it is an extension of his work.

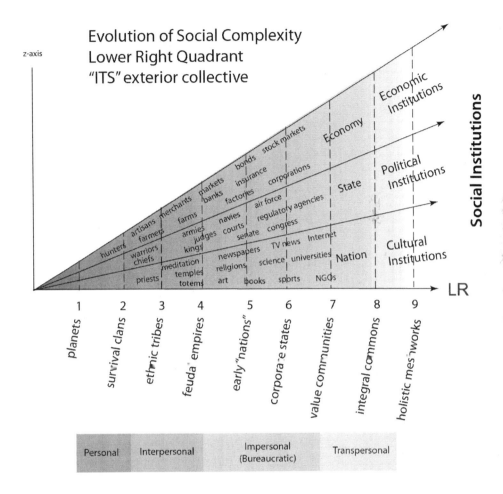

Figure 8. The External Evolution of Social Institutions in Three Spheres, Lower Right Quadrant, z-axis. © Gordon L. Anderson

Figues 6-8 provide a three-dimensional graphic framework of the evolution of human society.

SOCIAL PRINCIPLES AND SPHERES

There are three aspects to consider as societies evolve toward integral commons.

First, each social sphere—culture, economy, and governance—has different underlying principles. These principles are related to three aspects of social nature that are spontaneous in human life. They manifest as natural social products: language, money, and law. They represent the natural desire to live peacefully with others. Human institutions that destroy or impede these natural social orders are destructive of human life and the pursuit of happiness.

Second, institutions that arise one social sphere are dysfunctional in the other social spheres. The pursuit of money does not produce good culture. Culture is grounded in the pursuit of truth, beauty, and goodness. The economy is based on the ownership, production, and exchange of goods and services. Governments do not invent or produce. They are based on force. If they force people to love, work, or buy a product, they suppress natural pursuits and cause frustration, anger, and resignation. The proper role of the government is to use its power to act as a referee, allowing everyone can pursue happiness freely, so long as they do not harm others.

Third, each stage of social evolution develops from the previous stage. This is the evolutionary nature of human society. Social institutions are created by sovereign individuals. When they violate individual sovereignty by exploiting, manipulating, or abusing their people, they undermine their long-term existence. Social revolutions that try to eliminate all the traditions and social structures they stand upon often get sent back to the early stages of evolution and have to start over. Some revolutions have led to a return to barbarism. Evolution transforms; it does not destroy.

FREEDOM AND ORGANIZATION

Integral society is not organized by force but evolves to enable human individuals to live free, happy, and better lives. It allows individuals to pursue good and discourages or prevents them from causing harm to others.

An integral approach must distinguish between spontaneous order and planning. Spontaneous order is unplanned, undesigned, and emergent. It arises from human practices, norms, and institutions that are products of human action but not human design.[1] They arise freely. Steven Horwitz explains that Hayek saw this as placing limits on planning:

> For Hayek, this concept was central to his critique of "scientism," or the belief that human beings could control and manipulate the social world with the (supposed) methods of the natural sciences. The concept of spontaneous order provided a framework for seeing that social institutions not only could emerge without human design, but that they worked better when they did so.[2]

Each organization has a specific mission, and that mission will drive its culture and organizing principles. Leadership requirements for organizations are different depending on the mission. Giving instructions and managing people's performance on a job in a factory is necessary for the efficient output of quality products. An employee knows and accepts this in taking the job. However, using one's position as a leader for sexual or financial favors or the imposition of religious beliefs on employees violates personal sovereignty and freedom.

The principle of *voluntary* membership is essential for any organization that imposes commands on members to achieve the organization's mission. This principle has become routine in cultural and economic institutions. People are free to join or leave. It has become a constitutional right as "the freedom of assembly."

However, membership in a state is not optional. The purpose of a government is not to impose cultural values or produce goods. In serving this end, it has no right to *command* people to pursue its institutional ends. Instead, it's role is to restrict behavior that would harm others. Employees in a government are voluntary members and subject to their superiors' commands, but government should serve and protect its citizens, not command them.

---

1. Steven Horwitz, "Is the Family a Spontaneous Order?" *Studies In Emergent Order,* Vol 1 (2008), p. 163.
2. Ibid.

THE FAMILY AS THE PRIMARY SOCIAL INSTITUTION

The family is a unique biologically-based social institution arising spontaneously arising from human reproduction. Children would die without the care they get from their families until they can live independently. Chimpanzees and other mammals also create families to raise their young. Families may take on various forms, extended, nuclear, or without the father present. Their primary biological mission is child-raising, not marriage. Parents or guardians are responsible for all three social spheres in a family: teaching knowledge and values, teaching skills of self-independence, and instilling social rules.

Marriage is a common social construct that provides orderly responsibility for child-raising and a social constraint on sexual behavior that prevents disruption and harm to other families. Thus a family is a mixture of spontaneous order and social planning.

Schools and other social institutions like scout camps have emerged to supplement primary care-givers in socializing children. They can teach general skills like reading and math, survival skills in nature, specialized skills for producing goods and services, and the rules of good citizenship in the larger society. However, these institutions are primarily instructional, and the behavioral patterning process is largely completed before children attend such social institutions.

Such institutions have a role in facilitating happiness in adults by navigating the spontaneous orders of language, the market, and the law and enabling the personal pursuit of truth, beauty, and goodness.

THE SOCIALIZATION OF ORGANIZATIONS

There is a parallel between the socialization process of individuals and socialization processes organizations. Integral society requires social institutions to develop to maturity in fulfilling their mission. The socialization of individuals for interdependence and mutual prosperity replaces the animal instinct to steal and fight for existence. Social organization also have to learn how not to steal or harm others.

It is easy for people to use social organizations as vehicles for self-en-richment, ideological goals, and other activities that redirect their mis-sion. Since the rise of early states, nearly all social institutions have arisen to address spontaneous needs, only to be later hijacked and side-tracked by the second or third generation of leaders for ulterior motives. The founders of organizations have a clear purpose in mind when they orga-nize them. However, those who follow often see institutional positions as a job, a means of employment, self-enrichment, or vehicles for some other goal.

Organizational cultures, rules, and mission statements should curb these impulses to misuse organizations. When this is inadequate, gov-ernment actions are needed to curtail the activities that are harmful to members of society. The Constitution of the United States stands out as an effort to curtail the abuses of earlier state governments, protecting the sovereign rights of citizens against rulers who would oppress them for political and financial gain. It is an attempt to socialize government better, but more improvements are necessary for integral society.

Religions, family businesses, and a few social clubs were the social organizations existing when the U.S. Constitution was ratified. Today, corporations, financial institutions, political parties, labor unions, public utilities, and many other organizations have a strong impact on individ-ual sovereignty. The U.S. Constitution did not address these future insti-tutions and required vigilant citizens to curb their abuses as they arose.

Some laws and agencies do curb newer types of institutional abuses. However, the abuse of social institutions has expanded more than been contained. Today, most new laws serve moneyed interests and social institutions in ways that support the enrichment of elites at the expense of the taxpaying citizen.

Governments are not the only social institutions to be misused. Corporations, banks, charitable foundations, universities, pharmaceu-tical companies, and a host of other organizations exploit people when they are not limited to their mission and refereed by good laws. Like indi-viduals need to be socialized in communities, social institutions require socialization into an integral society.

ACKNOWLEDGMENTS

I would like to acknowledge those who have contributed through collegial work in the study of society and governance institutions. First is the late Morton A. Kaplan, Distinguished University Professor Emeritus at the University of Chicago, who envisioned a set of comprehensive academic conferences on world social systems. I worked with conference chairs: Alexander Shtromas, at the Hoover Institution, on the Soviet System, Ilpyong Kim, at the University of Connecticut, on the Chinese System, and Edward Shils, at Cambridge University, on Liberal Democratic societies.

Second, I would like to thank those in the field of integral studies with whom I collaborated: Allan Combs, who arranged for me to be an adjunct professor at the California Institute of Integral Studies, Ken Wilber, who advanced integral theory, and Steve McIntosh, whose books on *Integral Consciousness* and *Developmental Politics* develop the field of cultural evolution parallel to economic evolution in this book.

Next, I would like to thank Professor John K. Roth for advice, the late Professor Nicholas N. Kittrie for constituional law, and Professor Don Trubshaw for the development Institutional Value Theory and institutional resiliences. Dr. Norman G. Kurland contributed the ideas of binary economics and the just distribution of capital.

I am grateful for practical institutional experience by heading the finance committee of the board of trustees of the University of Bridgeport. Conflict of interest, institutional hijacking, and government interference is widespread in higher education.

Finally, as a member and president of the board of the Legislative Evaluation Assembly of Minnesota for over 20 years, I witnessed the erosion of constitutional processes and the hijacking of the state government by political parties and the administrative state. Many of these same methods of government hijacking are used in federal legislation and need to be constitutionally restrained.

INDEX

U.S. Declaration of Independence 88,
145

V

Vanguard, investors 72, 152–153
Volker, Paul 119

W

Washington, George 103, 148
Weimar Republic 111
Wilber, Ken ii, xii, xiv–xv, xx, 2, 36,
61, 63–64, 98, 104, 135, 138,
160–162, 168
wokeism 72
World Economic Forum 132, 137

Z

z-axis 162–163